Stupid George!

the Big Fat Loser!

STUPID GEORGE!

the Big Fat Loser!

George W. Childress, DMD

Exceptional Press
LaGrange, Georgia

Published in 2023 by Exceptional Press.

ISBN 978-1-61027-759-4 (paperback)
ISBN 978-1-61027-758-7 (hardcover)

Exceptional Press
114 Calumet Center Road
LaGrange, Georgia 30241
george@drchildress.com

Interior design and production by Quid Pro, LLC.

Stupid George!

the Big Fat Loser!

PROLOGUE

Tarnished but Transparent

I explained to Carson that hiding in Mr. Huff's garage was not a good idea. In fact, I believe I introduced the term trespassing! "I'm not trespassing, I'm waiting on Mr. Tim to turn on the waterfall."

Realizing I was about to fight a losing battle and Carson was big enough that it would hurt me to drag him back home, I backed off the futile negotiations and told Carson I hoped Mr. Tim didn't call the police or shoot him. Carson's response, "He can't call the police, he can't shoot me, he has to turn on the waterfall." With that, I retreated back to safe territory, cracked open a beer, probably uttered a prayer such as "God help me," and waited for Carson's next steps.

After about 15 minutes, I could hear Carson emerging from the Huff garage and soon realized he was coming down our driveway, not a happy camper. At this point, I had begun to realize to pick my battles and quickly retreated inside the house after shotgunning the remaining beer. I felt this way I could at least preserve the glass in the front doors as I knew they were about to experience category 5 hurricane force.

As Carson approached the front steps I opened the doors and praised him for coming home. He immediately started to run upstairs and turned to me and with all of the pinned up emotion he shouted, "STUPID GEORGE" ... and if that wasn't enough, when he got to the top the stairs, he reiterated, "Hey Stupid George, you BIG FAT LOSER!!!"

In the days ahead my father, Parker, who was 90 years old, fell and broke his hip. I was sitting in the ER with him that night and he and I both knew this would be a tough event for him to make a full recovery considering his underlying health concerns. I respected and loved my father dearly and he was the greatest Christian male influence in my life. He was tough, gruff, grumpy at times, but full of wisdom, and always had an opinion! He could laugh too. I looked him in the eyes and asked him if he had any words of wisdom for me. He said, "Don't do anything to tarnish the family name." He and I both smiled and I thought to myself, "Well, I am Stupid George, the Big Fat Loser!" I asked, "Assuming it is too late for that, what else you got?" He softly but firmly said, "Take care of your mother and suck it up and move on." He did not have much to tell me after that and died six months later.

As for my mother, Ruth, she was the greatest Christian influence in my life. As the father of four children including one with autism, I struggled with the balance of trying to check on aging parents and in-laws, and raising children. I have an incredible wife and extended family that helped assure my parents and in-laws were well taken care of during their declining health. In one of my final conversations with my mother, I guess I was complaining about someone else's behavior, and my mom's response was simply, "Well, George, aren't you glad you're not the judge! Why don't you just focus on loving them!"

Well, I began this way because it proves that no matter how great a foundation is laid before you, it is up to you to continue the legacy or destroy the legacy. The story I'm about to tell you is true, on-going, painful, but hopeful. It is the story of Stupid George ... tarnished but transparent.

Purpose

This book is a simple attempt to chronicle the struggle of an inept dad adjusting to raising, loving, and living with a child with autism. Through faith in Jesus Christ my Lord and Savior, prayer, humor, red wine (sometimes tequila and bourbon), and the Holy Spirit I have survived so far (When I began writing this book I was fifty-five). Just as important if not more is the rock in my life named Mary Lynn, my wife of thirty-two years. The child is Carson Childress. I am Stupid George, the big fat loser! Well, sometimes I'm called Dad, but most of the time I'm George.

As I sit here typing these words, Carson, now seventeen, is repeatedly asking me when Mom is coming home. "In two days Carson, she is at a meeting in the mountains with Allison and Caroline and will be home Sunday." Carson replies, "George, can we go eat today?" I reply, "Tomorrow we will go see Drake but today we will pick up my fishing boat." Carson, "Ok, but Mom is coming home in two?" "Yes, Carson, she is coming home in two (days)," I said, repeatedly reassuring him that consistency would return to his world. Confused yet? Or does this sound like conversation in your home? I realize I am blessed that Carson is verbal and mobile and can take below reasonable care of basic needs with assistance. I look around every day and see other special needs situations and realize we are blessed with the abilities he does have as opposed to what he doesn't possess. Nevertheless and selfishly, this is a transparent true life story of *my* struggle as a dad with a boy with autism.

Apologies

To Carson: I know why God has Mary Lynn in your life and I have learned why you are in my life. But for the life of me I can't figure what God was thinking when He chose to put me in your life. With your sisters and brother, my parenting tactics were seemingly successful but with you these tactics set the stage early for a deep wedge between us that is taking a long time to remove. If autism could have been shouted out, spanked out, or forced out, you would be cured now. I'm sorry for every time I shouted mercilessly at you, hit you, dragged you, and was hateful in anyway. I can never take those times back but I certainly would if I could. I still struggle with how to be your dad and make each day the best I can, but right now I'm just focusing on adjusting on how to be a positive impact on both of us and our family.

To Mary Lynn: You know how I have failed many times as a father and husband but your love, devotion, and discipline have helped me so much over the years. Thank you for being my accountability partner and I'm sorry for disappointing you when I have. I still dig you like I did when I first met you, and my love is deeper every day for you! (More on this love story later.)

To Allison, Drake, and Caroline: I'm sorry for not being the best Christian influence in your lives as your father. My temper and impatience have impacted all of you in negative ways at times, but please know I love you with all my heart and would do anything for you! Along with your mother, y'all are the best thing that ever happened to me and to Carson!

With the previously mentioned confessions, I know Department of Family and Children Services has a good case against me. In fact, I have often thought they should offer a Friday check-in facility just like Andy Griffith offered Otis in Mayberry and allow potentially abusive parents a chance to just lock themselves up until they are ready to face the world again. I'm not sure when the statute of limitations expires on abuse but I might be reading this book from a jail cell if it is ever published. I do not want to make light of child abuse, as certainly I know it is perverse and rampant in our world. However, I do sympathize with families of special needs children and especially single moms or dads that are struggling with the stress in their life.

We need to remember that these children are not evil or intent on disobedience, but often their behavior is an attempt to escape their pain or a situation that is bothering them. That is where the struggle lies, what is the difference between neuro-typical misbehavior and non-neuro-typical misbehavior and how do you as a parent deal with it? If you know of a single parent dealing with a special needs child, please offer support or at least check on their support system ... I promise you they need it! They may be a duck — smooth on the top but paddling like hell underneath just to keep moving forward against the stream of life!

So enough of that, and again, this story is about me, Stupid George, not someone else! My hope is that you will laugh, cry, be mad, be glad, and experience every emotion that life offers as you read this story. But I also hope and pray that if you are reading this story as a parent of a special needs child that you will find hope and an assurance that you are not alone ... God has you in the palm of His hand; although you may feel that you are at the edge!

Keep paddling, my ducks, God has you where he wants you at this time! If anyone is offended by this story I have asked to be buried face down so you can kiss my ass anytime you want to come by. Don't give up on me yet, please keep reading.

My Mantra

Re-boot Day: 2-8-2016.

Carson is fourteen years old and we are in the prime of hormone surge and establishment which is wreaking havoc on everyone. Nonetheless, I felt prompted for some reason to write the following words. I titled it "re-boot day" because my IT guy always asks if we have re-booted the computer when a problem occurs and this often "fixes" the issue. My consultant tells me sometimes you have to "blow-up" (figuratively, not literally) your systems to get a fresh start.

I have learned through this process that I only have one problem ... a child with autism. However, I now consider that a blessing! I only define it as a problem because true problems can't be fixed by money. Everything else is simply an issue. Issues are things I worry about or spend a lot of time thinking about. Most of my "issues" now have a system, process, or accountability piece that will ratify, clarify, and multiply in a positive way!

Because of this process, I am developing a sense of contentment that God has me where he wants me and all I have to worry about is being the best steward of what he has entrusted me with in His kingdom. I will always be driven and have a desire to win, but it is only because I want to live each day striving to live up to my God-given potential.

I will fail at times and often, but that is where grace plays a key role in contentment ... that God is there (whether I fail or not to live up to that potential) ... and through Jesus Christ my Lord and Savior I will spend eternity in Heaven.

When I First Knew

Looking back, I can't tell you when I first recognized that Carson wasn't exhibiting neuro-typical behavior.

I know what you're thinking, "Big word, George, for such a simple mind!" But that is the word I quite often hear in the professional realm describing Carson, actually "non-neuro-typical." All I know is, he ain't wired like I am. Some of you will respond, "Thank God Almighty!"

I do know that at a very young age, probably nine months or younger, Mary Lynn expressed some concerns that he was not doing some of the same things that Caroline, his twin sister, was doing. For example, Caroline would make and maintain eye contact longer than Carson when you engaged with her. General developmental steps just came quicker for her. Often times it was suggested that boys just develop slower than girls, "So don't worry about it, he will develop normally at his own pace."

One thing I have learned through many years of marriage to the same woman: Trust that motherly instinct and female intuition because they are usually correct; and if they are not, just keep your dang mouth shut. I also knew Mary Lynn was highly educated regarding early childhood development and as part of her master's program she had done some research and observation of kids with autism ... but autism never entered my mind.

Beginning with hearing test and other diagnostic tools, we embarked together to get to the bottom of it and set him on the right path! After a couple of visits with professionals in pediatric development, I began to come to agree with Mary Lynn that something wasn't right with Carson compared to his other three siblings' development.

My earnest prayer became, "God heal this child and let me know what I need to do as his earthly father." I just knew my prayer would soon be answered just the way I wanted and we would be on the path of throw and catch, hunt and fish very soon.

It all came crashing down on me as Mary Lynn and I spent one afternoon in Dr. Leslie Rubin's office (a well-respected developmental pediatrician) where Carson was observed and evaluated. He told us after a couple of hours that Carson had pervasive developmental disorder not otherwise specified (PDD-NOS). To make a long story short, that meant autism without the big label!

Very confidently, he said, "George and Mary Lynn, you can't immediately fix this and he likely will always struggle in some way, but you can develop a program that can lead to tremendous development ... but you have to be proactive!" He laid before us a path to begin intensive therapies, some of which were extremely helpful and some of which led to dead ends and frustrations. I believe most people in the medical and developmental field truly have a gift from God and do everything in their power to practice in the best possible way what is best for their patient. Dr. Rubin was no exception. He was patient, wise, and compassionate and wished us well as we began this formal journey.

I privately cried, cussed, and asked God why, but openly said to myself and others, "Suck it up and move forward." Other than bowel movements, nothing productive gets done sitting on your ass.

The best advice was early intervention with occupational therapy and we saw the most development with this over the years. We may discuss later all the other treatments, diets, and interventions, but I think Mary Lynn would agree that early OT is key. (I'll correct this later if she disagrees.)

If I could do it over I would support Mary Lynn more in her concerns and act sooner rather than later. If your gut feeling is something is wrong, get opinions and not just one.... This leads to more educated decision making.

Bath Time Then and Now

Mary Lynn has always tried to "watch her figure" and after the birth of four children I especially appreciated her discipline! By the way, even after 32 years of marriage I can't get enough of her.

Less I digress, after the twins were born she went into "walking mode" to get back into shape. Her walks were long and well deserved and usually occurred in the early evening, quite often after dark. Her walking partner at the time was Andrea Trainer. Someone once asked me if I worried about their safety on the walks as their walks often took them downtown. My reply was that I pitied the fool that attacked them.

While she was gone, it was my task to bathe the twins and have them in bed or ready for bed. By this age they were able to sit up in the tub without risk of drowning! Obviously, efficiency over effectiveness was my goal as well so the quicker the better! If I felt like time was not of the essence, I would run the water and let them have a soak bath.

Carson did not particularly enjoy bath time, so he became a priority to get done first! He would cry and often cry loudly during bath time so I felt like the best way to get through it was to hurry! In this effort, as the water was running I would bathe him while the tub was filling up! The more he cried the faster I bathed. No sooner was he in a full soap suit would I move him under the running water and rinse him off. Now, if you are envisioning water boarding, this was far from it as I understand the method. I was careful to not let it run in his face so I would turn him backwards and rinse his hair, just as anyone would. The crying screams would continue and I would forge on until finished.

Meanwhile, Caroline was enjoying herself in the other end of the tub and likely wondering about all the commotion at the other end! No abuse occurred during this time but as I recall the noise from Carson would have indicated so! It was at this time that my mind did begin to wonder if something was different about Carson. Mary Lynn had made a few comments about eye contact and differing developments compared to Caroline, but I had dismissed them and just said "difference between boy and girl" or "he will catch up."

Was this the first time I felt as if something was wrong? Hindsight is 20/20 but I do think this was the first time that I really felt like there might be an issue. Later, after the diagnosis, Carson began to have intentional therapy sessions and his OT tried to explain to me sensory processing disorders.

Carson's initial aversion to running water and the noise of the water in the tub was likely an early sign of some type of sensory integration dysfunction. If I could do it differently, I would make bath time a more intentional time of relaxation trying different things to help him adapt to the needed bath. Perhaps I would do a sponge bath just like when he was an infant. Little did I know that as a seventeen year old he would take at least two to three baths a day *voluntarily* and swim like a *manatee!*

Dookie and the Marks

I need to tell to tell this story and get it over with because it still haunts me to this day. It is one of the lowest points of my human existence.

Carson was potty trained so I'm guessing he was at least four or five years old. I don't remember what age he potty trained, but I do know that accidents were more common and it took longer than our other children. Mary Lynn knew he couldn't go to the next class up at St. Mark's if he wasn't potty trained so that had become our next milestone of developmental achievement.

I had just gotten home from work and a trusted family friend was supervising Carson and she said Carson had just gone outside. Apparently, it had not been a good afternoon behavior wise. She said he had not been very compliant. I looked out and he was squatting on the back patio near the pool doing #2! Quickly and fiercely, I became enraged and embarrassed by this endeavor on his part. I don't know why he did it and he couldn't explain why he did it, but I certainly was not going to tolerate this animalistic behavior. I picked up a stick and began spanking him with it and some of the strokes went across his lower back.

Fortunately, I realized I was out of control and stopped after a few whips. Carson was screaming and crying and I looked around and the care giver had tears in her eyes and was walking away to leave. She never commented to me about it but I know she was disappointed in my actions. I realized I had made a grave mistake and had not only left marks on my son but scarred him on the inside as well. I truly believe this one act drove a distinct wedge between me and Carson that I am still trying to overcome today.

When Mary Lynn returned home, I immediately told her what happened and she saw Carson's back. She immediately burst into tears and told me *my* animalistic behavior was way beyond Carson's actions on the patio. She was right of course! There is no humor here at all to tell, just a sad and tortuous moment for Carson and my relationship. I acted out of anger and there is no excuse.

Why? No excuse, I guess I just felt like I had to respond immediately to his behavior and violated a cardinal rule of discipline ... NEVER DO SO WHILE ANGRY! I pledged soon thereafter to never lay a hand on him again.... I wish that pledge had held true. Unfortunately, I have battled anger and temper most of my life and continue to struggle at times. Fortunately, Carson is physically tough and a quick healer. Total transparency here is going to lead to judgment and ridicule of me as a person and parent. I totally accept that and respect anyone's opinion.

What I truly regret is how Carson must have felt toward me ... that "the man in my life, my Dad, who says he loves me so much and so often, who prays for me and to me, could treat me like that; who is this guy?" Sometimes, the ones we love the most, we treat the worst.

So, what did I learn and what would I do differently? I would have cleaned up the "project" and told Carson that was not appropriate of course and loved on him and then moved on. With autism, discipline is different and takes many moments of patience and calm response to change behavior because the processing mechanism is different for these children. They don't tend to be mean or spiteful, but sometimes the stubbornness and aggression is their mechanism for communication that something is not making them happy. I'm sure he had a motive. Perhaps it was because he knew I was home and he wanted our friend to stay instead of me. Perhaps he thought #2 was just as acceptable as #1 outside. Like all boys and most red-blooded male adults do in the backyard, we certainly had practiced peeing in the bushes and seeing how far our stream could go. Maybe he wanted to see what kind of "brown art with a DQ swirl on top" he could create beside the pool. Whatever the motive, all he learned was that the most dominant male figure in his life could be a monster.

While I believe in spanking (while under control) as a last resort for discipline, we all know that any type of discipline without careful thought and while angry can be abusive and excessive. I don't know if Carson still remembers that day or not, he never brings it up, but I know I do! Of all the parenting mistakes I have made, that one is definitely a top 10. Please forgive me, Carson.

Whitesville Road Drop Off ...
He will grow out of this, right?

Starting at the age of 3, the public school system has a program for early intervention for developmentally delayed children. Mary Lynn was very aware of this program and in true momma bear fashion had been plotting a plan for her man cub! He and Caroline had been in a church preschool program since the age of 2, so this would be the first time they were separated due to developmental differences.

Immediately upon turning 3, Carson was tested for this program and found to be eligible, although he had passed the earlier speech test and hearing test that are often used as screening tools. Again, it was that momma bear instinct and Mary Lynn's intellectual expertise that was leading our path to help Carson.

I can't remember the reason I was elected to take him that day, but it was likely that Mary Lynn and I were having to split the drop off duties due to separate locations for the first time with the twins. This story is not long or particularly humorous. In fact, it still evokes sadness when I reflect on it.

Carson and I entered the classroom and I took a look around at several different children and it hit me that my child was now part of the "special class." I don't mean this in any insensitive way, but this was not the badge of honor I had hoped and prayed for Carson. While I am thankful that many wonderful early intervention programs are available, I think most parents would agree that they would rather be able to take the "normal" path to development as opposed to the "special" path.

The teacher was extremely sweet, understanding, and encouraging. With the encouraging aspect that I perceived from her, I asked how many times she witnessed children grow out of this pathway. Hoping she would say, "quite often" or "all the time," I was shaken by her apprehension to answer my question. While she continued to be encouraging, she said that "it does happen" but more often than not this is a "long but steady process." As a fixer, this is not what I wanted to hear.

As I left the building to get into my truck, I felt a sense of impending doom and helplessness. As I began to drive off, a wave of tears began to flow. For those of you who know me, this is not unusual for me but this time it was different. Reality was setting in that this was not a quick fix for Carson and that we were in for the long haul.... I had no idea.

More importantly, I was no longer in control (not that I ever was), and I could not fix my son! I pulled off to the side of the parking lot so I could continue my pity party. I did try to pray for comfort and a peace that passed all understanding, but I have to admit I was still upset when I started driving to work. Nevertheless, it was time to "suck it up and move on." Looking back on it, this is where we formally started our intervention journey and our "special path."

Carson, Where Are You and the Atlanta Zoo?

One of my challenges has been and continues to be to find activities that Carson and I can engage in together. One weekend I decided he and I would travel to the city (Atlanta) and stay in a hotel room. The plan was to stay in a hotel with a view of the night lights, swim, order chicken fingers, fries, and honey mustard. I'll have to admit that red wine was on the list as well for Stupid George, but only to be enjoyed poolside or during a movie Carson and I rented.

I called ahead and received expedited check in so that we could go straight to our room and not have to wait in line. All was well as we pulled into valet parking, quickly exited the area and made our way to the room. No lines, no whines, everything was just fine! Upon entering the room, Carson immediately took off shoes and shirt, but retained his shorts!

He was comfortable, content, and satisfied with the view from the room and full access to any video he wanted via wifi and his iPad. Then a small snafu occurred when Carson notified me that his battery was dead on his iPad and he needed his charger. No problem, I thought, as I had packed a charger and was totally prepared for any and everything. I had already unpacked and just uncorked the wine so this would only be a slight distraction and easily remedied. "Where in the hell is the charger? I know I packed it!"

Then it dawned on me that we had been stuck in traffic getting to the hotel and we had to charge his iPad in the truck. In my haste for a quick entry to the hotel and room I had left the charger in the truck. Ok so no problem! I called down to the desk to see if someone could retrieve it from valet and bring it to the room. "No problem, it will be up shortly."

Now keep in mind that patience is not a virtue that people with autism possess. I told Carson that the charger cord was on the way and that satisfied him for about 4 minutes as we gazed out the window and watched the city transition from daylight to dark. I called back down to the desk and was told that there would be a delay because they had a large number of guests checking in and they would bring it up as soon as they could. Typically, this would not be a problem, but I had a non-typical issue with a 14 year old with autism.

Carson was escalating with anxiety and frustration which I knew would lead to anger and aggression. I couldn't take him to the lobby with me because of the crowd and the unpredictability of Carson's response to the lobby traffic and no charger! Not to be dramatic, but I had an escalating situation where I didn't want to have to pay a damage deposit and the red wine would soon run out! I resorted to pray for intervention and developed the fortitude to make a parental decision. I would have to get the cord myself. "Carson, we have to get the cord out of the truck, come on let's go!" Now remember, for people with autism, most everything is literal, so saying "let's go" meant leaving and not coming back; especially in his heightened state! He wanted to stay and I had to get a charger somehow. So I resorted to praying again and felt like I had to make a run for it. "Carson, I'm going to get the charger, so stay in the room."

We were on the 18th floor so taking the stairs was NOT going to happen. I quickly went to valet and told the attendant I needed my keys to get something out of the car. He gave them to me and I went to the car but no charger! As I was headed back to the lobby I ran into the original bellman and he told me he left my charger at the front desk! I went by the front desk and retrieved the charger and went back to the room as fast as I could. Upon entering the room it was eerily quiet. Carson wasn't there! I called for him but no answer. Panic set in quickly but I also figured there were only 28 floors to the hotel so he had to be in the vicinity!

Remembering that Carson for some reason preferred to go up stairs as opposed to down, I went up one flight of stairs and called for him, "Carson, where are you?" Quickly I heard, "I'm right here, George. Do you have my charger?" He was standing by a window in the hallway looking out at the city lights ... why he couldn't do that in the safety of the room I have no idea. Nevertheless, the rest of the night went well. Chicken fingers were ordered and consumed and movies were watched.

Earlier, as we were stuck in traffic trying to get to the hotel, Carson had noticed an interstate sign showing the Atlanta Zoo and had remarked that he would like to go to the zoo. I said sure but didn't believe for a minute that he would go or bring it up again. As we were about to go to sleep and the lights were turned off, Carson said his prayers and after Amen, he asked if we could go to the zoo in the morning. Again, I said sure but knew that when we woke up I would take him to Krispy Kreme for donuts and head back to LaGrange.

We awoke early and he was ready to go as I anticipated, but I felt a sense of accomplishment and gratitude that we had a successful outing, just the two of us. After we ate our donuts, Carson said, "Ok George, let's go to the zoo!" Now I knew I was pushing my luck but I thought, "why not?"

I quickly went online and purchased two tickets to the Atlanta Zoo. We were the first to arrive in the parking lot as the zoo didn't open for another forty-five minutes. At this point, the trip could've gone bad but a series of minor miracles occurred that still today I believe God just wanted me to know to never give up on what Carson might accomplish. First, as we approached the gate to get in it was still closed and Carson would have to wait in line. Also, he had to use the bathroom and if other times were any indication, he wasn't going to wait. A zoo employee had noticed us earlier and asked Carson if he was excited to go in. Carson said not really, he just needed to tee-tee! Anyway, the worker was close to the gate and noticed the despair on my face and granted us immediate entry fifteen minutes early and showed us the nearest restroom ... miracle #1.

Carson had two things on his mind at this point. First the crocodiles, then the pandas. The crocodiles were on the way to the pandas so we stopped in the reptile center first and checked off the crocodiles (which may have actually been alligators). Our zoo trip was going exceptionally well! People were beginning to come in but it still wasn't very crowded. There was a slight line for the panda exhibit. Carson waited patiently and we were able to see the pandas without incident ... miracle #2.

His mission was accomplished and he told me he was ready to go to the truck. As we headed back through the zoo, he spotted a ropes course that I have to admit looked like a blast, but I never dreamed Carson would attempt it. "George, I want to do that." I said, "Carson, you will have to wear shoes and you only have flip-flops. He said he would do it if he could wear his flip-flops. Interestingly, the same worker we met at the front of the zoo was working the zip-line that morning. He noticed Carson and me discussing the zip-line and he told Carson if he would wear my tennis shoes and put on the "3 point harness" he could do the zip-line. Without hesitation, Carson kicked off his flip-flops and let me put the tennis shoes on him ... miracle #3.

Immediately, Carson set off on the ropes course without assistance. He navigated beautifully with minimal instruction and I began to weep at what my son was doing on his own. The worker noticed me getting emotional and he said this was not a surprise to him as he sees kids with special needs do this type of thing quite often. The fact that the gentleman was where he was at the moment and was there for Carson and me will always feel like an angelic appearance to make a special moment ... miracle #4.

At the end of the ropes course, about thirty feet in the air, a zip-line hung between Carson and the end of the course. The last time Carson had been that high was when he fell through our attic over twenty feet and miraculously only fractured his humerus. He was very apprehensive to step off the ledge for the zip-line but after some encouragement he did it and completed the course ... miracle #5.

When he came down, he said, "That was so much fun!" I asked, "Would you like to do it again?" Carson replied quickly, "Naaaahhhhh, let's go to the truck and go home." And that we did!

As we traveled home I thanked God for granting me that time with Carson and his cooperative spirit and enthusiasm at the zoo. If I could do this all over again the only thing I would do differently would be to pack multiple chargers! Stupid George felt pretty good about himself at this point but reality was just around the corner.

Lesson learned ... enjoy the milestones and keep praying for the next and stamina in between!

Tupelo to Memphis

Salvation with our Lord and Savior Jesus Christ is the most important decision in life to me. As my mother once said, "To know that my children have professed their faith in Jesus Christ is the most satisfying feeling I could have as a parent."

I know God is a compassionate God and has all this worked out, but sometimes I do contemplate how He handles the people who can't seem to make conscious decisions to follow him due to mental delays or cognitive disabilities. Now I know I'm setting myself up for righteous criticism from those who believe in an *all*-inclusive God or no God at all, but again I remind you this is *my* story, not yours.

Carson has been exposed to the Gospel, but to our knowledge has not made a "public profession of faith" as we like to call it in the Baptist church. Nevertheless, I know he has Jesus on his mind at times and in his heart. For example, the family had embarked on a driving vacation (all six of us) that would take us through Tupelo, Mississippi, and of course early in the trip I had made several references to God and Jesus but not always in the most reverent tone.

One question I have often asked is, "If you say 'God' and there is clearly a five-second pause before you say 'damnit,' is that considered blasphemous? If you say, "Jesus Christ, Drake, would you please shut up!" Is that considered using the Lord's name in vain? Just asking, because between a neuro-typical son that I'm pretty sure started talking immediately after passing through the vaginal wall and a non-neuro-typical son that would scream at you when you were not in the left lane when a passing lane was present, my nerves where shot by the time we passed Cheaha Mountain in east Alabama. Sorry for the digression but you need to understand the circumstances.

As I was saying, our first official stop for sight seeing was going to be the birth place of Elvis where we would see the house where he was born and raised in Tupelo. The first night we had planned to spend in Memphis after touring Graceland, so it was only fitting that a nice southern white family would stop and pay respects to the birthplace of the king (of rock and roll) on the way to Memphis. No disrespect intended for Jesus the King of Kings or Martin Luther King, Jr. Obviously, it gets geographically confusing when referring to all these kings, but Carson soon made it clear which king he was not going to see.

As we pulled up to Elvis' childhood home Carson was visibly and audibly already upset because we had detoured off the 4 lane and he was not ready to stop. Mary Lynn in her soft and compassionate tone said, "Look Carson, this is where the king was born." Without hesitation and through reddened cheeks and tears, Carson said, "I can't see Jesus!" We all started laughing loudly and this did not help the situation. I'll never forget leaving Tupelo and the birthplace of the king (of rock and roll) navigating back to the interstate while dodging flying debris from the back of the SUV as Carson hurled any lose object he could get his hands on!

As I raced down the ramp to enter the interstate at like 95 mph, Carson pressed the lock on Caroline's seat and pushed her seat as hard as he could forward. The momentum forced her into the back of Mary Lynn's seat with near blunt force trauma to her head and neck as if we had hit someone head on. In case you doubt this scenario, it is well documented on video camera somehow within the car with complete audio. The main things you can hear are Carson screaming and Allison laughing hysterically at the scene. There may be a somewhat muffled phrase as well ... (God (five-second pause) damnit, Carson!') Forgive me, God (and family).

The most disturbing part of this trip was to come the next day. We went to Graceland and Carson would have none of the tour so Mary Lynn and I sat in the parking lot with him while Allison, Drake, and Caroline toured Graceland. For the afternoon, we planned to tour the Civil Rights museum and sights associated with Martin Luther King, Jr. We were driving around the motel where Dr. King was assassinated and driving at a slow pace so as to find parking or at least give the sight the reverence it deserves. Carson was escalating in his displeasure of the slow pace and my compassion and patience were at an all-time low towards Carson at this point. After he hit and bit one of his sisters, I found the nearest vacant parking lot and in lightning speed parked and pulled Carson out of the car before Mary Lynn could lock me out of the car. What ensued was a fisticuff between Carson and myself with my anger and lack of self-control getting the best of me. I lost control. If a German Shepherd and a water hose would have been present and the color of his skin darker, it would have been reminiscent of the civil rights days and the shameful behavior of the whites towards the blacks.

Thankfully, I could hear Mary Lynn shouting in the background to stop and looked up to see the girls crying and begging me to stop. Shameful, I know, believe me I know, but I told you I wouldn't hide the ugly truth. I'm also shameful of the abuse the black race endured as people snapped in anger and prejudice. The damage has been done to Carson and the damage has been done to the black race. All I can do now is apologize, learn, love, and move forward and pray that my actions never again escalate to that level. We all need to love one another, learn from our mistakes, and move forward with love for *all.*

As for lessons learned from this trip I would have to say that I would leave Carson at home next time ... but then again this chapter would not have been written. I certainly would try to control my language, get out of the car *by myself* when angry, and understand that the rigor of a vacation with constantly changing scenery and historical objectives may not be the best situation for a child with autism. Give me the beach and a drink please!

Mrs. Angel … An Angel with Delusional Paranoia

In the course of writing this book, I have mentioned and will mention several people that have greatly impacted our family through this journey with Carson. Some will be mentioned briefly in one-line sentences but one in particular deserves a complete chapter all to herself.

Mrs. Angel has impacted many families over the years as a childcare provider both in the public sector and through individual care in families' homes. If you have ever experienced Mrs. Angel's soft spoken words and love for her families that she worked with, you know exactly what I mean. All four of our children were exposed to her at a young age through church daycare or mother's morning out programs. However, when Carson and Caroline were born we utilized Angel on another level! She became part of our family and we love her as if she is family.

As it became more and more clear that Carson's issues where of a persistent nature, it was clear that Angel had a gift for dealing with him while also making Caroline feel like she was the only one in the room...a true gift! Several years went by and Mary Lynn and I felt very comfortable leaving the kids with Angel so we could get away for a a day or two for some "personal relationship time." (I always advise parents whether of special needs children or not to remember that you had each other first! Keep nurturing YOUR relationship as well while being a parent.) It was not always easy for Mrs. Angel while we were away, but she never seemed rattled or discouraged when we returned. Needless to say, we felt like God had blessed us with an angel during this time with Angel. What God giveth, can also be taken away.

The story goes like this. For the past 25 years, Mary Lynn has graciously made it possible for me to attend a boys' golfing weekend with some guys I went to dental school with and have remained very close over the years. It is a time for personal reflection, relationship building, and very little fun. (HEHEHEHEHEHE) When I return, Mary Lynn usually has a story to tell me about the weekend that she feels would have been better had I been present.

For example, one night I was gone and a bat was discovered in our bedroom flying around. Mary Lynn bravely handled this with grace and poise I'm sure and she somehow coaxed the bat out of the house. It was likely best I was not present as there likely would have been much sheet rock to repair from a shotgun blast attempting to kill the bat. Another time away Carson's sister, Caroline, experienced her first car accident and Mary Lynn handled this with grace and poise all the while dealing with Carson at the same time!

The ultimate George absentee story involves Mrs. Angel. In the middle of the night, Mary Lynn awoke from a deep sleep to our door chime sound which we leave on in case Carson decides to leave without telling anyone. She knew it was highly unlikely that he would leave at 4 AM so the anxiety level ramped up immediately. According to her, she called out, "Caroline, is that you!" No answer but she could clearly hear someone foraging around the house. "Caroline, is that you!" No answer but by this time Mary Lynn had made her way to the hallway and could see a figure in the dark. "Who is there?!," she exclaimed. *No Response!* With all the bravery, and I'm sure poise and grace, Mary Lynn flipped on the light and there stood Mrs. Angel in her pajamas and hair rollers! "Mrs. Angel, what in the world are you doing here, it's 4 AM! "I'm sorry Mary Lynn, did I scare you?" Mrs. Angel said. "They told me to come on over to the house." Mary Lynn said, "Who told you to come on over?" To make a long story short, Mrs. Angel was suffering from delusional paranoia and "voices" were instructing her to do irrational acts.

Obviously, our angel now needed our help. We informed her family of the events and Mrs. Angel was able to get access to the help she needed. Our angel was now gone but not forgotten. We continue to pray and check on her periodically to be sure her needs are being met but can no longer depend on her as a Carson "sitter." For the time she spent with our family we are forever grateful.

There is no good way to end this chapter as this story is sad on several levels, but I find humor in Mary Lynn's comments when she called me the next morning after the 4 AM visitor. "George, Good morning! How was your night?" "Great! The guys and I had a great time telling stories and laughing a great deal. I slept great!," I replied. Mary Lynn, in all her poise and grace, "Just know this, I'm not making this crap up, George...."

Lessons learned from this experience are that everyone has a story and we need to be attentive to the needs of everyone around us as much as possible. Also, Mary Lynn needs some weekends away as well!

Teachers

Teaching Carson in a classroom has always been a monumental task. Mary Lynn and I always felt that if you had a Childress in your class, you were blessed! I know that sounds arrogant so let me explain.

By blessed, I mean you were going to have a well-behaved child, respectful of others, maybe a talker but responds to correction; supportive parents and a room mother that would throw a party that rivaled none! When Carson entered formal classrooms we began to notice the collateral effect of him being in a classroom. Retirement, relocation, reassignment, and possibly refusal became an obvious trend after having Carson in a regular classroom.

Mrs. Crews ... loving and caring tutor, retired. Mrs. Ann ... early intervention teacher so loving and nurturing and now retired. Mrs. Mayfield ... pre-school teacher always with encouraging words for Mary Lynn despite challenging days, retired. Mrs. Norton decided to go back to school in special ed ... miraculous!

Mrs. Moore ... kindergarten teacher we told to treat him like any other child! Disastrous approach for us to recommend. Retired! Mrs. Harlin ... moved to Colorado prior to the legalization of weed. Mrs. Trainer ... dear friend and master of the modification of classroom assignments: to this day when Carson sees Mrs. Trainer he states, "Trainer, I can't do any work!" ???

Mrs. Doerr had the "privilege" of being a neighbor and teacher for Carson, so loving and sweet to him all the time, even at 9 PM when he shows up to "borrow" a video from her house. She went into administration! Mrs. O ... life of the party and allowed me to come observe my sweet angel in the classroom. Upon arrival Carson stood up at his seat and said loudly, "Hey George, how are you today! Everybody say, bye George!" I left soon thereafter and Mrs O is still an incredibly positive and hilarious lady but she is now *retired!*

During elementary school we were advised to keep Carson "mainstreamed" as long as possible. However, looking back I can't say this was the best approach. If I could do it differently now, I would *insist* on a consistent one-on-one paraprofessional with Carson to help him navigate his day.

Additionally, we likely would encourage a more inclusive sensory environment for most of the day to accommodate his sensory needs during the elementary years. Sensory Integration Dysfunction or Sensory Processing Disorder in my humble opinion is the most underappreciated and underestimated element in many behavioral situations, especially in children. I am no expert as I have already proclaimed, but any occupational therapist will most likely give me five stars for this comment! If you are not aware of SID or SPD, then Google it.

An example could be for you and me to sit in a chair in a room with lights on and a teacher talking. One of the light fixtures has a slight buzz coming from the fixture but our ears tune out the buzzing noise and we focus on the teacher. For someone with SID, the buzzing noise can be like finger nails on a chalk board which overwhelms the sensory system and triggers a fight or flight situation or simply a "fidgetiness" that is interpreted as ADHD. Certainly, this may be an oversimplification of SID, but many classrooms could be modified with simple accommodations to make for a more comfortable learning environment for many children on the spectrum.

Middle school was a disaster and has its own chapter.

High School was a breath of fresh air when Amy Brown was Carson's teacher and Arthur was his behavioral technician. We finally were at peace most days with Carson at school. Thank you to Mrs. Snyder and Coach Williams for helping Carson to finish his high school years successfully. Consistency and predictability were the key!

Diana

Diana ... the little Diana ... the little firecracker with a heart for Carson the size of the sun.

Diana was the exceptional education teacher at Carson's elementary school. While Carson was still in the mainstream classroom he began spending significant time with Diana for one-on-one instruction and modified teaching. Little did we know, but this connection would become the catalyst for connecting with Carson at school.

Many families with a special needs child will tell you that at some point a single individual entered their life and it was a game changer. Finally, we felt like someone was beginning to understand Carson and connect with him on an educational and behavioral level like we had not seen before. No offense to anyone else, but Diana had a gift with Carson and he slowly but methodically developed trust and love with her that was unparalleled and perhaps hasn't been duplicated even today.

Diana was able to calm Carson when others could not. Diana was able to teach Carson when others could not. Diana was able to engage Carson when others could not. Diana provided consistency for Carson that others could not. Diana was a God-send!

Fortunately, we were able to reconnect with her for one year in an otherwise disastrous middle school experience and this allowed us to make a more deliberate decision regarding high school and how those years should play out: consistent one-on-one behavioral technician and in a self-contained classroom that provided Carson stability and predictability.

While we spent many years trying to force Carson to be mainstreamed in a classroom, the later years were much more effective for him with this individualized attention with the same behavioral specialist in a consistent environment. I don't know if we had agreed to this earlier that it would have made any difference, but I do know that a consistent paraprofessional in the earlier years would have likely been more effective in Carson trusting the school environment. Thank you, Diana, for advocating for us and encouraging us to insist on this change.

To this day, Diana and Carson have a special connection. Quite often, she will come stay with Carson while Mary Lynn and I go out to eat or take a day to get away. He is always so excited to see her and it gives us great comfort knowing we are leaving him in such caring and capable hands. Diana is an angel with Carson, but it is my understanding that at a baseball game she can quickly grow horns, especially if her sons were playing. I also know that if she knew at any point that Carson was being mistreated she would grow horns as well!

When it comes to teaching a child with autism, it comes as no surprise that consistency and stability are keys to minimizing behavioral incidences. No doubt a learning objective should be for individuals to develop coping mechanisms to navigate the world but first there must be a level of trust in the provider which begins with consistency and predictability. Diana has provided these traits for Carson and also has a gift of connecting with Carson (along with many other students in her career) like no other person except his mom. Two people Carson would do just about anything for are Diana and Mary Lynn ... consistent and predictable in his eyes.

His Prayer Life and My Faith

According to Hebrews 11:1, "'Faith is confidence in what we hope for and assurance about what we do not see."

Although I have many shortcomings, as an adult I have had many conversations with God ... prayer! My faith in God is my centerpiece on a table of dysfunction and imperfection. Stupid George is really just like you in that he is struggling to make sense of an otherwise chaotic world. I know God created the world, and when he put humans on the earth we have done all we can to abuse it and take it for granted. My faith keeps me grounded to the point that I know God is in control and will ultimately heal us all and gather us into His kingdom if we believe in Jesus Christ our Lord and Savior. Now, what does this have to do with Carson and this book?

As I mentioned, I have consistently been a man of prayer asking God to help me be a better person and not be a poor witness for God's kingdom. Obviously, based on some of the stories already mentioned and the ones to come you certainly have the right to ask or think, "How could a praying man of God act in such a cruel, insensitive, and harsh way toward a child with special needs?"

It's simple, I'm stupid George, the big fat loser!

Before my children were born, I prayed for their health, their futures, and for me to be a Godly influence in their lives. As Carson was diagnosed, I began to realize that one of these prayers was unanswered. My Faith was not shattered but I must admit I asked God why. Again, not why Carson is in my life but why am I in Carson's life?

I continue to pray daily for the veil of autism to be lifted and for me to experience a conforming and consistently cooperative Carson ... but it ain't happening! At this point, social awkwardness, aggressive behavior, severe anxiety, and repetitive actions still dominate Carson's day and leave me with a knot in my stomach.

Maybe this is why Carson is in my life ... he keeps me humble and constantly relying on God's strength knowing I can't fix the problem, and in God's infinite wisdom He has not healed Carson.

In the meantime this is what I do ... I keep praying for strength, compassion, discernment, and wise choices as Carson's father.

In the meantime, this is what Carson does: every time he eats he prays: "God is great, God is good, let us thank Him for our food. By His hands we are fed, thank you God for our daily bread. Amen."

In the meantime, when Carson goes to bed and when he is on his way to school, "Dear God, thank you for this day. Thank you for Mommy, Daddy (sometimes George), Allison, Drake, Caroline, and Carson. Help Carson to have a good day. We love you Jesus. Amen."

I'm not sure when exactly he began to pray these prayers, but I do know they are deeply entrenched into his routine ... mostly because of his mom and the Holy Spirit!

According to Hebrews 11:39-40, "These were all commended for their faith, yet none of them received what had been promised, since God had planned something better for us so that only together with us would they be made perfect."

I don't know what the earthly future holds for me or Carson. I do know that it appears unlikely that the veil of autism will be lifted from him. However, I will continue believing that God has a plan for Carson, God has a plan for us all. I just need to cling to the faith of knowing I may never see my prayer answered on my terms but that I can find peace and joy in each day and that Carson can too. My faith remains strong knowing that God will provide healing for Carson in His time!

Just Follow the Plan

Individual Educational Programs (IEP) and Behavioral Intervention Programs (BIP) are key components for communication among educators and therapists involving children with developmental delays. The pathway to developing these plans are labor intensive, time consuming, and humbling for parents. However, when done properly and with detail, they are an invaluable tool and certainly a highly legal and enforceable document.

As a teacher, Mary Lynn was well aware of the benefits and necessity of the IEP. She had the ability to empathize with the teachers having to develop the plan and also the tenacity of a mother to be sure the plan was modified and tailored specifically to Carson's needs. The biggest challenge during elementary school was consistency of a paraprofessional to help Carson navigate his daily routine and transition from year to year.

One thought process among some administration was to change the para-pro annually so that Carson was not dependent on one person. In hindsight, this was detrimental as no consistency was in place and Carson was continually adjusting to new authority figures which can be a challenge for a child with autism. The IEP has to be continually modified as needs arise and no one should be afraid to ask for things to be added or deleted during modification periods.

When behavior is a problem, a behavioral intervention program is developed to address problem behaviors or actions that may lead up to problem behaviors. As I have discussed, Carson has struggled with aggression his entire life so a BIP has been a part of his program since late elementary school. A problem began to manifest in middle school where Carson was growing in stature and his aggressive episodes became more destructive. For example, if Carson didn't earn his computer time, he would knock the computer off the desk. Obviously, this is destructive and disruptive for the classroom even for special needs classrooms. When the principal tried to intervene and say this wouldn't be tolerated, I agreed but said what does the BIP plan state. Interestingly, the principal seemed unaware that a BIP existed for Carson.

After consultation with an ABA (Applied Behavioral Analysis) therapist and a discovery of situations that would lead up to the behavior, it was discovered that if the BIP was followed these behaviors would decrease ... and by the way, the behavioral therapist wanted to know why the computers were not bolted to the tables! When the principal wanted to know how they should respond to Carson, my response was: learn, implement, and follow the BIP. The BIP plan also led to Carson eventually being assigned a behavioral technician who became the single most positive impact on Carson's behavior and development.

This happened after an incident where Carson had his finger mashed in a door and a well-intentioned and dear lady who was not his para-pro tried to console him, he pushed her back, she lost her balance, fell, and broke her arm. This was extremely unfortunate and we felt so bad. Fortunately, the lady was understanding to us as a family and a BIP plan was in place. Once we demonstrated how the BIP was not being followed, we were able to successfully have a behavioral technician assigned to Carson. Out of a potentially bad situation, some good came out of it! We had been advocating for this for some time with no success.

My comment to the administration was how much more risk are we willing to take before a major lawsuit occurs from an ill-trained or ill-equipped employee or a child is hurt in a situation that could be avoided. In conclusion, never give up, continually refine the programs, and be sure the programs are being implemented.

The most successful people with Carson have been the ones to study the past, be flexible in the now, yet follow the proven protocols. The process of frustration led to our introduction to Mr. Arthur Edwards: another God-send for Carson and us.

Arthur

If I could sum up why Carson was able to stay in the school system it would be with one name: Arthur Edwards.

Arthur came to us during one of our darkest moments in Carson's educational journey when Mary Lynn was emotionally spent from receiving negative report after negative report in middle school. Carson's behavior was off the chain in middle school and no one could seem to make a connection.

We had made the decision to minimize transitions by placing Carson in the "special education" program with the hope that this would minimize the negative behaviors. However, the environment and schedule were new: school, teachers, para-pros, classmates, etc. Daily, Mary Lynn would get behavior reports of desk being knocked over, classmates pushed, Carson screaming, and computers pushed off tables. Something was triggering this behavior but no one could connect the dots.

Introducing Mr. Arthur Edwards, a "behavioral technician" recommended by Ashley Paré, a BCBA (Board Certified Behavior Analyst) contracted by the school system to evaluate Carson.

Instantly, Arthur made a connection with Carson. I don't know if it was Arthur's size, skin color, or his calm but firm presence but he connected with Carson. The problem was that while Arthur was brought in to stabilize the behavioral situation and help train para-pros on how to handle Carson, Carson was having none of this. He was connected to Arthur.

After a while, the behavior reports began to be more positive although each day had challenges for sure. Instead of Mary Lynn getting a barrage of how bad Carson was that day, Arthur would pick the positive development to report. As for any negative behavior, it was acknowledged but Arthur would calmly state, "It's not anything I haven't seen before and we will continue to address and extinguish behavior." These positive reports were instrumental in encouraging Mary Lynn and me to continue the public school journey. As I said, a connection was clearly forming between Arthur and Carson!

Long story short, it was determined after three para-pro attempts which resulted in reassignments or resignations, Arthur should be Carson's full time one-on-one. I will give the school system credit for finally agreeing that consistency in the para-pro was important for Carson's school day. More importantly, for some reason Arthur agreed to take the task on full time! You need to understand that Arthur knew nothing about LaGrange, and would commute daily from Auburn and eventually Atlanta, to guide Carson through his day.

Arthur is a well-educated, former serviceman who I feel put his "career" aside for a time to make a huge difference in our life. You see, Arthur was the single most male influence in awakening me to how to deal with Carson. If Arthur had been present in our life early with Carson, Stupid George may not have existed! Arthur taught me (and I was a terrible student) the appropriate way to respond to Carson. The best response to Carson's aggression was no response ... total opposite of a Stupid George response. Granted, I continued to fail but I was able to witness a behavioral expert come alongside Carson and help shape his days for the positive.

I wrote earlier of my Christian faith and that has not wavered. Explain to me why God uses an African American Muslim male to influence me for the positive! Narrow-minded you say? Absolutely! But that is also what is at work here. Not only is Carson becoming a young man dealing with his autism in more positive ways, but I am maturing as a grown man in acceptance and compassion towards Carson and the people around me. "Loving your neighbor as yourself" is becoming a living picture for me. Now if I just won't screw it up!

Mary Lynn

If Arthur is the most influential male to me in my journey with Carson, then Mary Lynn Childress is definitely the most influential female to me in my journey with Carson.

I will never be able to put in words how much she means to me, but I definitely know why she is in Carson's life. She is the most patient, disciplined, loving, compassionate mother that any son could imagine. I don't know how much he comprehends his relationship with Mary Lynn, but I know he desires her approval and demonstrates his love to her above any other person.

I know you think that she is his mother and that this just comes natural. No! This relationship is supernatural. Mary Lynn allows God to carry her through each day with strength and compassion. I have seen her cry (not often), angry (but not sinful), and hurt both physically and mentally, but I have *never* heard her say a hateful or hurtful comment about or to Carson. This is strength, people: supernatural strength!

Not only has she had to deal with Carson's behavior, but she has dealt with my outbursts, impatience, and stupidity. She has been an example and a rock for me during this journey. And while I have tried to be a rock for her, reality reveals I have been more like a dirt ball that dissolves under stress.

Nevertheless, I am thankful every day that God put her in my life and based on Carson's daily prayer he is thankful as well! Mary Lynn reminds me often that God has a purpose in all this and we just need to be obedient to God's calling to be Carson's Mom and Dad. She certainly is a living example of that obedience and sets an example for me to follow. Now I just need to live it!

Twin Sister and the Siblings

I have written already regarding Carson's mom and her number one influence on Carson.

A close second are his siblings: Allison, Drake, and Caroline, his twin sister! They have witnessed a lot of life with Carson and me, and how they have turned out to be the exceptional people they are is a testimony to Mary Lynn and her mothering instincts. I love them with all my heart, but they have been easy to love ... most of the time! Most importantly, they have loved Carson unconditionally and treated him like a brother no matter what the circumstances. Even though he doesn't express it outwardly, I know he cherishes them and knows they are part of the inner circle that can't be broken. Just like mentioning Mary Lynn in every prayer, he mentions Allison, Drake, and Caroline in each prayer as well.

Caroline has received the most aggression from Carson since she was "closest" to him. Just like her mother, I have seen her cry, hurt, and angry, but I have *never* heard her say a hateful or hurtful comment to Carson.

One of the most treasured pictures we have is one that has *all* of us present when Allison and Bo got married. Mary Lynn's one request was that after the wedding guests had left the church, she wanted a picture with Carson in a tux with the family. When I heard this I immediately felt guilty for knowing I would have to consume a lot of alcohol in church to tolerate this request! Nonetheless, the wedding was successful and I maintained my sobriety through the ceremony knowing full well what was to follow.

Diana was staying with Carson as we had made the decision to not have Carson be part of the ceremony and risk a fire in the sanctuary from thrown candles or broken stain glass from when any object was thrown like an old bouquet! Diana had promised Carson she would take him to Zaxby's, but on the way she informed him that Mary Lynn wanted them to stop by the church and take a picture with the family. I met them downstairs as they came through the door. When he saw me with the tux, he said, "Not that suit! No George!" Knowing that my wife and beautiful daughter were upstairs waiting for this picture, I began the process. Well, as I bent down to help him put on the pants over his boxer shorts he caught me with a right hook to my temple that staggered me! Since Diana was there as a witness, I couldn't hit back! I was able to complete the task but definitely needed an Advil and wanted some alcohol to numb the moment!

At that moment as we entered the sanctuary, everyone was already in place for the picture and God simply ordained that moment as Carson held Mary Lynn's hand for the family picture. The *second* the photographer took the picture, Carson came out of that tux like he was Magic Mike in velcro pants. Keep in mind, this is in the altar area of the First Baptist Church. (I will tell you this, every time we have an altar call now all I can do is visualize Carson there in his boxer shorts.) Just as quickly as he had taken the tux off, he exited the sanctuary in nothing but boxer shorts!

Fortunately, Diana had parked out front next to the awaiting limo and Carson was safely in the car. When I staggered to the window to praise him, he said he was sorry for hitting me, asked if he did a good job for the picture, and asked if he could go to Zaxby's now! And that they did ... thank you, Diana! When I went back in everyone was jubilant with what had transpired and I had a headache but felt a sense of prideful accomplishment.

A few years later, Drake married Sarah Beth and the decision was made for Carson to make a guest appearance via video in his tux. This time we were in the basement of our home to make the video and Arthur was present. You think I would have been on guard, but I'll be damn if I didn't receive the same right hook!

We accomplished the video and Arthur got a good laugh about me letting my guard down! When Caroline gets married I pray that Carson can be part of the ceremony, but if he is I will definitely wear a helmet!

What an example they have all been, but unfortunately they have not seen the best father example to Carson. Despite this, I know they have a more compassionate, understanding, and tolerant outlook to the world than I did at their age. At this point, Caroline is applying to graduate school to become an Occupational Therapist and I am quite confident her career decision has been heavily influenced by the impact OT has had on her twin brother.

The Fall

Children with autism are at least three times more likely to suffer a serious or fatal injury than neuro-typical children. I don't know how you totally "accident proof" your home for a child with autism, but basically it would involve no glass, no hard objects, no water, no containers, no steps, no uneven surfaces, no electricity, no gas, no stove, and basically NO FUN!

In or around our home we have had batting cages, zip-lines, trampolines (without net guards), swimming pool, lake, boats, jet ski, multiple floors, and gas fireplaces and fire pits ... not to mention a fully equipped woodworking shop! Interestingly, no severe accidents have occurred with any of our children regarding any of the above mentioned hazards. Well, there was one exception with the outside zip-line involving Caroline.

On the first day of summer after Caroline's and Carson's kindergarten year, I thought it would be a great idea for her to try the new zip-line I had constructed in the woods on the edge of the yard. I had carefully constructed an elevated platform at the beginning, and the end was meticulously padded with old football dummies so as to "soften" the impact at the end of the ride. Caroline did not even make it past the first 5 feet. As she left the platform her grip failed and she plummeted to the ground ... no more than 6 feet! The problem was she landed head first and against a "rock" that was only partially exposed in the ground. As I picked her up to reassure her during her screams and sobbing, I was sickened by the immediate flood of blood from the right side of her head!

The fall against the carefully disguised rock had resulted in a gash from her eyebrow down to the outside corner of her eye. Of course, as soon as Mary Lynn saw it she informed me that she said the zip-line was not a good idea and now Caroline would be scarred for life! Well, as with many head wounds, once ice is applied and the area is cleansed, the gash was not as long or deep as expected. However, it obviously was going to result in a noticeable scar. I grabbed my “medical grade” super glue and closed the area to begin the healing process. To this day, if you look at Caroline from the side you will see her beautifully profiled face with a distinct exclamation point near the border of her eye that is reminiscent of that fateful day.

Caroline had her share of medical crises as a toddler as well with two visits to Children’s Hospital involving emergency abdominal surgery and a severe E-coli infection that resulted in a month of severe illness. But this book is not about Caroline, it is about her twin brother Carson. Needless to say, if our twins had been born first, Allison and Drake might not exist!

Carson’s accidents have resulted in a cracked ankle, broken humerus, and several lacerations requiring sutures (that lasted only moments before being torn out!). Interestingly, Carson and Caroline have not only shared being carried in a uterus together, but they have also experienced emergency helicopter rides to Atlanta for emergency care, although not at the same time!

The first significant Carson injury came at my office. I was there working after hours and the kids were upstairs playing. Suddenly, I heard this noise coming from the back of the office that sounded like Santa Claus had fallen through the ceiling. I didn’t hear any screaming, but as I rounded the corner I could see Carson on the floor and Drake peeking down from the second floor through the new hole created in the ceiling! This fall was only 10 feet and Carson was alert and the only complaint he uttered was, “I’m sorry I fell, I hit my head.”

According to Drake, they were playing hide and seek and Carson had “hidden” in the unfinished part of the attic where there was no flooring. Apparently, when he stepped into the insulation area he quickly went from the second floor to the first floor. Being reasonably sure that no head injury had occurred, we still took him to the ER for evaluation. It was our first experience with an ER and I must say the staff was great.

Of course, it was recommended that Carson have a CAT scan and when he saw the machine the anxiety escalated! He was not sedated and had tolerated the visit exceptionally well up to this point considering the time spent at the ER. Carson kept stating he was not getting in that “washing machine.” At some point we signed a release stating we didn’t want to sedate him just to get the CAT scan since it appeared he was alive and doing very well. We returned to our home with strict instructions to watch him for concussion protocol. Fortunately, he did well with no symptoms but this was a wake-up call for what the future would hold regarding emergency or even non-emergency medical events!

Some time later, Carson was "playing" on top of the playhouse and instead of climbing back down, decided to jump down since apparently this was quicker! The vertical decent was a little over 6 feet and his only complaint was "my foot, my foot, my foot!"

Well, I didn't want to battle the ER protocol again, so we were fortunate to get into the local orthopedic clinic before they closed to have his foot evaluated. As expected he had a slight fracture in his foot but not to the extent that would require surgery. The doctor explained that a simple boot would fix the problem. I thought to myself, "This is going to be interesting being as Carson already had a preference of being barefooted versus wearing shoes."

After 30 minutes of nothing short of wrestling a small bear cub, we succeeded in putting an orthopedic boot on him and we headed to the car. We had no sooner started the ignition and Carson had unbuckled his seat belt and was doing his best Houdini imitation to rid himself of this boot. It only took two minutes and almost one rear windshield until he had accomplished his goal and hurled the boot to the front seat. Mary Lynn and I looked at each other with wide eyes and said, "Well, at least we have something to add to the (doctor) dress-up kit at home!" Carson demonstrated his toughness in the following days as he never complained but simply limped around the house.

Our immediate problem was that we had a trip planned in two days that would involve an airline flight with all 4 children. So now the challenge was not only how to navigate a child with autism through a busy airport but how to navigate a child with autism and a broken foot through a busy airport! We had decided that we would persevere and had come up with a plan that as soon as we arrived at the airport we would get a wheelchair to put Carson in, hoping he would cooperate.

The plan worked like a charm as Drake took command of the wheelchair with Carson. As we approached the security line that had a 45-minute wait (a nightmare with autism), the line monitor noticed the wheelchair with Carson and immediately directed us to the handicapped area where there was *no wait!* God was truly at work here as we had dreaded the security lines and due to Carson's injury we had no wait at all. There is always a silver lining ... at least that's what I keep telling myself.

Little did we know that the fall through the ceiling at the office was just a small rehearsal for a much bigger event to come later. The lesson learned from the office fall was that children are curious creatures and love to explore. Children with autism are curious creatures and love to explore as well, but don't seem to have the "danger near" sense that neuro-typical children may possess. Therefore, areas of your home that are unfinished and may be considered "harmless" are actually attractive danger zones and possibly death traps.

After the office fall, we had the area of the attic that was accessible closed off so no more falls through the ceiling could occur even if the attic was accessed again. At our home, we had a much larger attic with some very small unfinished areas, but the door had a lock on it that we kept locked at all times. However, Mary Lynn and I had discussed that we should "floor" the remaining part of the attic and I had floored "most" of the attic and felt that it was a safe place. The door was still to remain locked.

One afternoon as I was finishing up seeing my dental patients at the office, Mary Lynn called in a panicked voice and told me she had called 911 and Carson was laying on the floor after falling through our foyer ceiling! I told her I would be there immediately, and as I left the office the fire trucks and emergency vehicles were passing the intersection near my office. Little did I know but they were headed to my house for Carson!

All emergency vehicles including me arrived at the house at the same time, but of course I outran everyone into the house! I could not believe the carnage in front of me as pieces of sheetrock littered the hardwood floor and I looked up to see the hole in the ceiling where Carson had come through. But where was Carson? Instantly, I looked ahead and saw Mary Lynn attempting to comfort Carson who had somehow managed to get up and go to the couch.

Ok, I thought, at least he is conscious and can walk. You see, Carson had not just fallen through an average ceiling. This ceiling is over 20 feet tall and the floor is hardwood! The paramedics were amazed he was conscious but convinced he would have internal injuries, broken bones, and likely head injuries. It was obvious he had at least one broken bone as I looked at Carson. His left arm and shoulder were not visible from the front! It was a gruesome sight and obviously a severe fracture and dislocation of some sort. The paramedics were awesome with Carson and of course we had immediately informed them of his autism. There would be no local emergency room visit as they explained that the "air flight unit" would meet us at the local school yard to take Carson to Children's Hospital in Atlanta via helicopter.... And by the way, we would not be able to ride along due to space limitations!

After the helicopter lifted off, we immediately left for Atlanta in our car, over an hour away. Needless to say, all speed limits were severely broken that trip and we even passed a state trooper on I-85 going 95 mph. We did have our emergency flashers on, but he never attempted to stop us ... miracle #1.

When we arrived at the hospital, we were immediately greeted by the ER doctor who informed us that Carson was doing very well considering the height of this fall. The CAT scan revealed no head injuries and only slight internal bruising of the liver ... miracle #2. The X-rays did reveal a complete fracture of the left humerus but the orthopedic surgeon confirmed that no surgery would be needed ... miracle #3!!!!! He told us that a removable splint/sling would be placed and that it would naturally heal with the weight of the lower arm keeping the upper arm straight as long as Carson would wear the sling.

Quickly, I had flashbacks of Carson's boot incident and how quickly he removed the boot, never to be worn again! This fracture was more severe and disfiguring. The first time he took the splint off he quickly realized his upper arm would move like a cooked spaghetti noodle. Apparently, from the scream he uttered, the pain was a quick reminder that the splint had a purpose to help him and not hurt him ... miracle #4.

That is not to say that it was an easy road in the following days as the splint and sling were certainly aggravating to him just as it would be for you and me. Between diazepam and prayer, we made it. I'm not sure who took the most diazepam, but I probably consumed two for every one that Carson took! Mary Lynn was an awesome nurse and caregiver as always.

In the following days we tried to piece together what happened despite what we thought was careful planning. Apparently that day, one of the children had gone to retrieve something for a school project from the attic and "locked" the door. (As it turned out, the lock was actually faulty and while it appeared locked it was in fact not locked.) Apparently,

Carson had gone into the attic to explore. There was one small area near where the chandelier "winch" was located that didn't have a board over it. A human body could barely fit through there so why would I worry with the "special" cut board required to completely seal that area, especially since the door would remain locked?

And that is how Carson broke his humerus and experienced a helicopter ride to Atlanta. Incidentally, the flight nurse said she had never had to give a child so much sedative to keep him calm during flight! Carson's metabolism of sedation meds is incredible!

What is the lesson learned? You can visualize and conceptualize all the dangers around you and you certainly should ... but then think and review again what possibly could happen. Children with autism don't "sense" danger like other children do. It's hard enough to keep a neurotypical child from getting hurt! When you introduce autism into the equation, accidental opportunities are magnified. All the prevention in the world can still be broken in the blink of an eye. We have to constantly be vigilant about the environment and thus the mental and emotional toll begins to build for the parent to not only worry about development milestones not being met but the increased risk of physical danger to our child.

Accidents will happen, they are part of life. When one does happen, be careful not to judge the caregiver or family until all the facts are known. Also, if you know of a special need situation, offer to provide some supervision to give the caregiver a respite on a regular basis ... and be on your toes! Watching a child take off in an emergency helicopter is not fun, and expensive too!

The Manatee

If Carson has a mammalian counterpart, it is the manatee. When he swims he will dive for seconds and resurface for air and then dive back so gracefully that he doesn't even appear to be making any effort to swim. He learned to swim at a young age as all our children did. We felt this was a life and safety skill that should be learned ASAP, especially since we love the lake and beach. Fear was never a problem for him; in fact, he jumped off a high dive very soon after starting to swim.

On one of our trips when Carson was about 5 years old, we were at Disney and went to a pool at the hotel that had a giant water slide. Carson immediately went down the slide and when he came out of the slide he immediately went under the water and remained long enough that it caught the attention of the life guards. Before I could respond, their actions would have made an episode of Baywatch! Before they got to him, he surfaced and then went back under refusing to clear the area of other sliders!

When I sheepishly entered the pool to claim my child, I explained to the life guard that he had autism and this would explain the conversion from a manatee impersonation into a shark-like impersonation as Carson thrashed about aggressively as he was being removed from the pool! Of course, looking back I should have explained to the lifeguards Carson's expectations after he came out of the slide to stay in the area. They told me that if I had done that they would have accommodated my request and the crisis would have been averted. Nonetheless, quite a crowd had gathered to watch the skirmish in the pool!

As a family, we have always been water people. I have had a boat of some sort since I was a young teenager. Mary Lynn and I owned a boat before we owned a house. Priorities! Fortunately, all of our children learned to appreciate our affinity with bodies of water and always jumped at an opportunity to go to the lake or the beach. On one of Carson's first exposures to the beach, he was so terrified of the moving waves and noise that he paced as far back from the water's edge as he could get, saying, "It's ok, it's ok, it's ok, it's ok."

It was heart-breaking because he knew he loved the water and wanted to swim, but the noise of the crashing waves was a huge barrier to his joy. Over time and with gentle reassurance by his mom, he soon developed a love for the ocean ... but never the sand! He wants clean hands and clean feet, so he doesn't spend any time in the sand other than the walk to the water's edge.

Now, it is a problem getting him to recognize the danger of the surf and beyond. He will swim out over his head in his manatee manner and scare everyone to death! He even does this in winter months if we are at the beach. When it is warm, I easily swim out with him and with a life jacket so that if he needs me I can be of service. The best Christmas gift I ever received was a full wet suit that I take with me if we go to the beach in the winter. Not only does it help with floatation, but it also helps reduce testicular atrophy in the frigid water!

Carson knows that red flags mean danger, but it has been a battle to get him to understand the danger associated with a red flag; quite a difference from the terrified 4 year old that wouldn't go near the water's edge. You may ask, "Why do you risk going to the beach with him?" If you could see the look of peace on him when he is in the Gulf you would understand. Going to the beach is really the only thing that Carson asks to do that involves leaving the house ... other than eating! That is why we do it. Today, at the age of twenty, Carson and I were at the beach (in December) and the red flag was up. For the first time in his life he said, "We can't go in the water because the drown flag is up!" What a breakthrough! He went to the pool instead and swam ... in the unheated pool!

As for the lake, we enjoy time on the lake with Carson. The best boat "investment" we ever did was a boat that has a small "cuddy cabin" where Carson can go and be by himself when he wants. The activity he enjoys is riding on the tube behind the boat and we have had many happy hours watching him on the tube. It has become a great diversion from video watching especially during the long summer days! It was through a gradual exposure to the lake activity that Carson eventually asked if he could tube. Now, it is a common request during the warm months. He will still swim in the lake during the winter but doesn't ask to tube; probably because we take the boat out of the water!

Carson will comply with wearing a life vest while tubing, but when he is done tubing he wants to take the life vest off and swim back to the boat ... even in the deepest water. Even though it is freshwater, his manatee instincts kick in and he will dive out of sight into the dark water and resurface seconds later. This freaks Mary Lynn out, so we try to reserve this special activity for just him and me! He is an amazing swimmer but the water still holds hazards that we all have to respect, so obviously I try to stop the boat in familiar areas where I am somewhat familiar with the depth and underwater structure. I have prayed that God would provide an activity that Carson and I could enjoy together. We bike ride on a tandem bike, he rides in the golf cart when I play golf, but by far the best activity is boat time!

One particular day when Carson was 17, Caroline had joined us on the boat and Carson wanted to tube. Carson prefers to tube by himself so Caroline and I were in the boat. She loves to post pics of her and Carson (she is our social media queen), so she was getting plenty of good video. He tubed from our dock to Whitewater Creek and back to Yellowjacket Creek to the Eagle's Nest and shouted for me to stop the boat. Now please understand, the distance he tubed was several miles! I expected for him to "swim" back to the boat. Instead, he got off the tube and swam to the bank, pulled his swim shorts down and urinated on the bank, swam back to boat, got back on the tube and tubed back to the dock! Thank you Carson for not polluting our clean lake!!!! For people who know the history of West Point Lake you will find that humorous because for years the lake was known as Atlanta's sewage dump ... but the fishing was great!

West Point Lake is a beautiful lake, and I appreciate the backyard resource we have as an outlet for Carson and me to enjoy. Now, that was a memorable time that afternoon that left me with a feeling of euphoria because of the amount of time we spent together and also that Caroline was able to enjoy it with us! While Carson tubed, Caroline and I played loud music in the boat. The euphoric feeling was soon squelched when after we got back to the house Caroline and I went to pick up pizza but didn't ask Carson to go with us. When we returned he was upset and an aggressive episode ensued that resulted in something broken I'm sure. He can communicate what he wants but oftentimes doesn't handle it well if his desires are not immediately met. Another day in the life of autism ... tremendous breakthrough of positive activity that was overshadowed by the unpredictable behavior associated with autism ... damn it!

I am grateful that God answered my prayer to provide an activity that Carson and I could enjoy together via the water and boating and a simple tube and tow rope! I just have to remember to be sure the boat is full of gas, batteries are dependable, and his chargers are functioning for his devices. Otherwise, when he gets in the boat it becomes very small when the autism rears its ugly head!

Lessons or advice from the water are to teach your child to swim as young as possible. Children with autism don't recognize danger very well and water is a huge source of accidents for neuro-typical children and especially non-neuro-typical children.

Be sure to teach the child how to swim as early as possible to help minimize water danger. Also, as young as possible, continue to expose the child to activities outside the home in order to discover your activity connection ... and always be on your guard!

Golf

T-ball ... nope. Football ... nope. Basketball...nope. Soccer, come on Carson, all you have to do is run around and kick the hell out of that ball, surely you can do that!

Hitting the ball off of the T, not a problem ... running to third instead of first base, problem. Sitting in the dugout until it is your time to hit, problem. Football, just no. Basketball, won a state gold medal for free throws as a six year old in the individual competition, and then next year pushed the gold medal winner off the medal stand when we won silver. Basketball as a team sport? ... even the gym noise causes me anxiety. Soccer? ... close, but team sports just seem to bring out the worst behavior in Carson when we have to wait our turn to participate.

Sooooo, golf. Now there is a sport! Like many dads, my hopes were for my sons to enjoy sports as much as I do and this would be a source of connection and activities for us to do together until they hated me as middle schoolers and teenagers ... then as young adults we would become friends again and play sports together again! You know, the typical parent/child relationship cycle.

Not with Carson. Carson and I had tried most all of the recreational league sport options and you can imagine how that had turned out: disaster. I'm sure I looked like an overbearing butthole of a dad trying to make his son enjoy a sport, but honestly I was just trying to force him to engage in some way. Perhaps my intentions were good, but my methods were consistent with stupid George, the big fat loser. The stories regarding our recreation league and Special Olympic experiences could make for another book in and of themselves!

I have played golf all my life. You would never know it; I'm terrible and still measure the success of my round not by strokes but number of balls lost! However, I do enjoy the fellowship, challenge, swinging as hard as I can, and 3 beers per 9 holes. The beauty of playing golf with Carson is that I can pick times that the course is not crowded and we can play at our own pace. I don't have to worry about his engagement with other people, and if he wants to participate he can, but if he doesn't that's ok too!

I always offer to let him hit the ball but most of the time he chooses to "walk the path" or ride in the cart and eat popcorn. Either way, we have found an activity that we both seem to be able to enjoy together for an extended period that allows Carson to get out of the house in a different environment and enjoy the outdoors. I also get to enjoy a lifelong hobby that I'm terrible at but enjoy with my son.

One particular Sunday afternoon, Carson and I were on the course and we had just finished the fourth hole. We were riding in a cart that day and I parked the cart next to the fifth tee box and prepared to hit my tee shot. Carson was eight years old and we had "practiced" driving a golf cart with supervision at home, but by no means were we ready for independent driving ... plus that was against course rules! I offered for Carson to swing the club and hit a tee shot but he elected to stay in the golf cart. I professionally addressed my ball as if I was in the final round of the Masters, and as I began my back swing I heard the distinct sound of a foot pedal being engaged by Carson. By the time I could stop my swing and look up, Carson was headed across the elevated tee box in front of me! My language was not conducive for a Sunday afternoon but basically it involved God and for Carson to stop that doomed to hell cart!

Miraculously, he hit the brake and the cart came to a sudden stop just before it was about to go over the steep side of the elevated tee box down an 8 foot drop. Shwuuuuuhhhh!!! That was close!

"Carson, why did you do that! Get out of the cart right now!" I shouted. And with the most beautiful but mischievous grin and subtle laugh he got out of the cart while simultaneously pressing the foot pedal and running away from the cart. One of my eyes watched him run down the fifth fairway because he knew I wanted to whip his ass while the other eye watched in horror as the golf cart went over the edge of the 8 foot cliff.

As Carson continued down the fairway I knew he was safe as he approached the 150 marker where I had hoped to land my tee shot, so I focused both eyes back on the aftermath near the base of the tee box. As I approached the edge of the tee box I could not see the cart, but I was picturing in my mind the seconds as the cart left the edge of the box and I could see the undercarriage of the cart and some of the contents of the cart including the ice from my cooler begin to take flight. The ice resembled a hail storm as it cascaded back down over the horizon and the golf clubs looked like a launching of random primitive weaponry!

As I inventoried the contents that laid scattered on the ground, Carson was making his way back to the area since his phone was part of the carnage. First miracle was he was OK! Second was the cart was relatively unscathed and was sitting on all four inflated tires. Third, no broken clubs. The only casualty was the totally emptied beer #2 of 3 that lay on the ground hemorrhaging its final contents. Since we had finished hole #3, beer #1 was empty in the basket already. Thankfully, beer #3 was unopened and was safely placed back in the cooler with what little ice I could gather.

Mary Lynn would have been so proud of me because as Carson came back voluntarily I told him how proud I was that he came back. I ask him why he drove the golf cart and he could only say, “I’m sorry.” I was over my anger, I was thankful he wasn’t hurt, and thankful we could finish the round. To my knowledge, no one witnessed the incident, as it was late in the day and the course was sparsely occupied. As I hit my tee shot and got back in the cart, I felt a sense of accomplishment ... that Carson and I had connected for a moment, created a funny moment, and found a “sport” we could do together.

I grabbed beer #3 and as I opened it I was baptized back into reality with the effervescing foam of a fiercely shaken beer. But I was left with that moment of a direct look into my eyes, a smile from his face, a slight giggle ... a connection. At least he had looked me in the eye and smiled!

The Huffs

This chapter is vital on two fronts. Number one, it is important because it ties some of the stories together, especially the back story to how I received my name ... Stupid George, the big fat loser. Second, it singles out a family that has meant so much to us during this journey.

Many families and friends have impacted our journey and been an incredible advocate and ally for Carson, but one family definitely deserves a chapter for many reasons. If you know this family, you know them to be fun, social, and living life to the fullest but at the same time quiet, private, and unassuming. They are incredibly successful business people, extremely generous, but yet humble and request or actually prefer no acknowledgment. Not like me, I want it *all* baby! If I've got to deal with the shit, shame, and sorrow, then give me the glitz, glam, and glory! Don't get me wrong, I know they struggle too at times as a family, don't we all, but I also know they will give God the glory in the good times and bad ... and they love each other unconditionally. *And they love thy neighbor unconditionally!*

I Googled (years ago this would have read, "according to Webster's dictionary") the definition of neighbor, and this is what came up: "A person living near or next door to the speaker or person referred to."

Then, being the upstanding, Bible-believing, Jesus-Loving, trash-talking, alcohol-consuming Christian I profess to be, I Googled the biblical definition of neighbor: "To be a neighbor, according to Jesus, means to come alongside someone." As Christian Americans, we must remember that we are Christians first, and Americans second.

But wait a minute, what does America have to do with this story......well, my motto for this year is: "a little less judging, a lot more lovin'." Really, wouldn't this world be a better place if we just let God do the judging and whenever He says enough is enough, it's enough, and all we did was love more and more unconditionally! Hell yea! Nevertheless, if you combine the secular and biblical meaning of neighbor, in my opinion, and yes, Mary Lynn agrees, the definition of neighbor is: *Huff*. You've heard of "tough love," well, I'm about to describe "*Huff* love."

Tim and Laura Huff have been our next-door neighbors for over 15 years and friends for even longer ... but nothing can test, weaken, or strengthen a friendship more that living next door to one another, especially with 4 kids each, one of whom turns out to have autism. Our children have always been cordial to each other and some have been closer friends, mostly due to timing and age discrepancies, but everyone from the Huff side has *always* been accepting and loving to Carson.

Now, before anyone from the neighborhood gets their panties ruffled or grippy's snatched tight, let me be the first to say that *all* of our neighbors and friends in our neighborhood have been accepting, loving, and caring to Carson. Thank you to the Foodys, Doerrs, Jacksons, Hales, Crites, Martins, and the man that walks every morning who I wave to that lives about a mile away and Carson tried to get into his house at sunset to charge his phone, Wilders (Thomas especially), Burns, Arringtons, Harmons, Laniers, Brannons, and Doughmans for all the pizzas, "borrowed DVDs," and unwelcome intrusions into your homes when Carson came calling ... and I was usually supervising. Not one neighbor *ever* called the police to my knowledge, they just called Mary Lynn! But the Huffs definitely put up with the most Carson influence of them all!

Now remember, Carson has a fascination with water, especially running water. When we built our house we were blessed to be able to put in a pool and Carson has enjoyed that pool more than any family member ... from 25 degrees to 103 degrees. When the Huffs built their house, they were blessed to be able to put in a pool as well, but not just any pool ... this pool has a waterfall. But not just any waterfall ... a cascading waterfall that meanders along a rocky path for about 20 feet above ground that would put any waterfall this side of Dollywood to shame. Additionally, underneath the waterfall cascading down the rocks is a corresponding water tunnel slide that is basically a miniature version of Great Wolf Lodge waterpark. Why? Because they could, and their goal was to create an unbelievable experience for their family and friends ... and oh how gracious have they been in sharing this amenity.

Well, for a young boy with autism and no social filter or graces, running water and a tunnel slide next door was no comparison to my pool, heated or not. The minute Carson discovered the pool nirvana next door, he was hooked. It didn't matter what day of the week, what time of day, or temperature, if Carson wanted to go the Huff's pool, he went ... and believe me, we had many confrontations with him to try and convince him this was not socially appropriate. But Laura and Tim would *always* respond, "Carson is always welcome." Now you and I know what else they could say: "Hell no Carson, get out of here Carson, you're not welcome at this time Carson!" They would have every right to say that but never did I hear it.

They will never know how much this means and meant to Mary Lynn and me over the years. Sometimes it provided a few minutes of respite in an otherwise long day for Mary Lynn, but it always caused anxiety for Mary Lynn and me because we knew it was an intrusion into their privacy. But they never complained. The only time I can remember getting a phone call was one night they were having a private party and Carson could hear the festivities. Well, at some point he entered the pool area for his nightly swim but instead decided he would jump off the rock wall 6 feet high into the hot tub with a depth of 2 feet. We were aware he had gone to the Huffs and were secretly monitoring his moves, but we were just worn down from an hour of negotiation to convince Carson this was not a party for us.

Laura called not to complain that Carson was there, but to express concern that she could not convince him that what he was doing was dangerous. Bless her, because I know she didn't need that stress ... sweet Laura! As with most of Carson's exploits, he was not injured and he soon came home uneventfully when he was done with his swim at the Huff compound. This is just an example of the tolerance and patience they have exhibited over the years.

I gave all that as a back drop to this next story that resulted in the title of this book, "Stupid George! The BIG FAT LOSER!" Carson has rarely called me Dad or Daddy, but as long as I can remember he has called me George. At times it was George with scrunched eyebrows. Then it became and still is when he is mad at me, Stupid George! Rightfully so, I'm sure you will agree. And then, at the worst of times it is Stupid George, you big fat loser! Not sure where that came from because of all the hateful things I have said to Carson I have never called him stupid or a loser.

One day, I was in charge while Mary Lynn was taking a much deserved break. The Huffs were not home but as usual their garage door was open. Thankfully, the doors were locked. To Carson's credit, he had asked me if he could go to the Huffs to swim in the waterfall (keep in mind we have a nice pool too, but no waterfall), and I had informed him they were not home so it was not a good idea. He seemed to comprehend this rationale but soon thereafter, I noticed the house was quiet and Carson was missing. This was not entirely unusual under my watch, so I simply pulled up his phone locator to pinpoint his location. Sure enough, he was at the Huffs but it showed him in their house, not the pool.

I promptly marched over to the house and realized the doors were locked. I reconfirmed his location indicating he was *in* the house. So naturally, I began yelling through the closed door for Carson to come out. In response, I heard a faint voice as if someone was being muffled, "I'm right here George." "Where Carson?" I replied. "Right here in this room waiting on Mr. Tim to come home." Seems perfectly rational except he was hiding in the utility closet off of the garage with the light off. Now, Tim and I are both God-fearing but pistol-carrying men and both feel if a stranger is hiding in or around our home they likely will not leave unharmed, possibly in a body bag.

I explained to Carson that hiding in Mr. Huff's garage was not a good idea, in fact, I believe I introduced the term trespassing! "I am not trespassing, I am waiting on Mr. Tim to turn on waterfall." Realizing I was about to fight a losing battle and Carson was big enough that it would hurt me to drag him back home, I backed off the futile negotiations and told Carson I hoped Mr. Tim didn't call the police or shoot him. Carson's response: "He can't call police, he can't shoot me, he has to turn on waterfall."

With that, I retreated back to safe territory, cracked open a beer, probably uttered a prayer such as God help me, and waited for Carson's next steps. After about 15 minutes, I could hear Carson emerging from the Huff garage and soon realized he was coming down our driveway, not a happy camper. At this point, I had begun to realize to pick my battles and quickly retreated to inside the house after shotgunning the remaining beer. I felt this way I could at least preserve the glass in the front doors as I knew they were about to experience category 5 hurricane force. As

Carson approached the front steps I opened the doors and praised him for coming home.

He immediately started to run upstairs and turned to me and with all of the pinned up emotion he shouted, "STUPID GEORGE" ... and if that wasn't enough, when he got to the top the stairs, he reiterated, "Hey Stupid George, you BIG FAT LOSER!!!" Of course I immediately responded in the most mature manner I could manage given the circumstances: "Oh yea, well, you're an ASSHOLE!" It was at this point that he entered into his bedroom and *that* door experienced cat 5 force ... no broken glass, just hinges. At that moment it came to me, you can't make this stuff up, you have to write a book ... and there is your title.

Finally, I will end this chapter with saying that not only have the Huffs been so kind to Carson, they have been great friends to Mary Lynn and me. There is hardly a time, especially in spring and summer when the lake is the place to be that we don't get a phone call or text asking us to join them for a drink, conversation, and laughs. Many times we have to decline the invite or only join for short periods due to our circumstances, but they never give up on us! They always invite and love unconditionally. That, my friends, is neighborly *Huff love!*

So if I could end this chapter with any advice to a neighbor or friend of a family with a special needs child: be inclusive, be tolerant, extend the hand of fellowship. And if they say no, just understand but never forget them ... they notice.

The Hot Tub

When Carson was turning 16, we had come to the conclusion that obtaining a driver's license and driving a car was not an obtainable goal! For our other three children we had saved and bought them used cars when they turned 16. It was not so much to spoil them with their own car, but more of a convenience for us to not have to take them everywhere they needed or wanted to be. Seems like a practical parenting decision to me!

But a car was not going to happen for Carson, especially since attempting to teach him to drive a golf cart resulted in nothing more than heated debate between Mary Lynn and me. Carson basically preferred to run the golf cart over the curbs and off the road so he could "feel the bumps."

With Carson's love for water and his insistence on swimming even in the winter months in an unheated pool, we made the decision to install a hot tub connected to the pool with a small waterfall. The project was done relatively quickly over a 6 week period. When it was finally finished, we told Carson the hot tub was ready to be used and now had hot water in it!

He immediately went outside and stated, "Oh wow, it is beautiful. It is beautiful George."

"Carson, do you want to get in," I asked.

"Naaaahhhhh."

Wow, now that was a gut punch! Spent all that money (but not more than a used car value!) and all we get is "beautiful, but NAAAAHHHH!"

Such is giving a gift to a child with autism! Sometimes it's a hit, but oftentimes they are indifferent to the gift. You better have thick skin and shake off hurt feelings or you will walk around with your lip poked out in a pouting posture! Carson gets more excited over a new pair of short pajamas or a simple DVD than any other gift!

Fortunately, about an hour later, we noticed Carson put on his bathing suit and head to the hot tub! It was in his time and on his terms! When he immersed into that hot tub you could see the stress literally leave his body. He absolutely melted into that tub. It is most always a daily occurrence to find him in the hot tub if not multiple times a day enjoying the sweet sixteen gift. Mary Lynn and I have often commented that was the best money we ever spent in Carson's therapy! He does love it and *so do I!*

Now I realize that not everyone has access to a hot tub and I certainly realize that others may absolutely have a sensory aversion to water, but it does seem in general that warm baths with epsom salt are very calming and therapeutic to neuro-typical and non-neuro-typical people. So, take a plunge and let the stress wash away!

Carson's Heart is Through his Stomach!

I continued to find ways to try and connect and engage with Carson as he grew older and one such activity became our "men's night out." If he has any of my qualities other than my temper, he does love to eat! We often say that the way to Carson's heart is through his stomach.

Usually twice a week, Carson and I would go to a restaurant, just the two of us. We had our "usuals" such as Pizza Villa, Hog Heaven, Los Nopales, Cisco's, and the legendary Captain's Cove. The staff at these restaurants came to know Carson and knew the importance of predictability and consistency for Carson.

Our nights out served several purposes. One was to engage Carson in a "controlled' social activity with other people around. However, we would pick non-peak times and get a booth in the corner whenever we could just in case behavior escalated before the meal was over. It was not unusual for Carson to ask to go to the truck after about five minutes when the food had arrived. I would intentionally park close to the front so he could go to the truck and I could see that he was ok. The purpose of this was to help him develop coping skills for properly leaving an uncomfortable environment.

Another purpose of men's night out was to give Mary Lynn a few minutes, maybe an hour, of respite. Typically, she had spent the after-school hours engaging and supervising Carson until I got home from work so the least I could do was take him out for a while! During this time, Carson's behavior was beginning to escalate and he was larger in stature so there were times that the "men's night out" was becoming risky business.

Los Nopales is always a safe haven for Carson and the service speedy and predictable. He always orders the same thing: chicken fingers and fries with honey mustard and another one to go! But that night, he had a particular edge about him that I couldn't pinpoint. We had a booth near the back as usual, but he became fixated on the water fountain in the middle of the restaurant and only wanted to sit there, even after the food was delivered to the booth in the back.

Being the center of attention with a young man flapping his arms at the water fountain was not what I considered a fun activity for men's night out. Maybe I was embarrassed, maybe it bothered me more than any other customer in the restaurant, but I felt it my duty to encourage my son to stop the water fountain shenanigans and come to the booth to eat. Carson informed me *loudly* that he wanted to eat at the table near the fountain, in the middle of the restaurant. As if he wasn't the center of attention already, he certainly was now ... and of course I felt like all eyes were on me to see how I would handle this young man and his disruptive behavior.

I began calm negotiations simply trying to reason with Carson that our food was already at our booth and he should come and eat it – or would he prefer to get it to go. I was certainly hoping he would choose to-go containers and we could get the hell out of Dodge and I could finish my margarita in the truck. While Carson was standing beside his table, I was standing beside my booth contemplating my next move or verbal coercion phrase.

Suddenly, Carson grabbed the corner of the table and flipped it like it was doll furniture. My immediate reaction of course was to run to him and of course his immediate action was to run from me. He was shouting, "You can't hit me George," to which I was replying, "The police have been called due to your behavior and we better get out of here!" I guess you can envision the scene. I was able to pin him to the floor and restrain him before he lashed out at anyone or flipped another table. When I looked up I realized that a nice family was sitting next to us looking in horror as to what would I do next. There was only one way out, through the front door.

Prior to the flip and chase, I had come to the conclusion that this wasn't going to end well and had laid enough cash to pay for the meal and tip and pay for the family next to me whose meal we had ruined. With all my might and energy that I could muster without spewing the half-digested quesadilla that I had begun to eat, I lifted Carson off the floor, wrapped his arms behind his back as if I was conducting a citizen's arrest and charged for the front door. He was screaming, I was about to vomit, and how we didn't shatter that door when we went out I don't know. Well

I do know, because at the same time an old friend, Michael Stogner, was entering the restaurant and realized what was going on and he opened the door for us as we came screaming through. I had momentum and didn't let go of Carson until we got to my truck and this massive amount of dueling white sweaty humanity collided with the door of my truck.

I quickly unlocked the truck and somehow got Carson into the truck and shut the door ... both of us screaming now! Michael had followed behind us and asked me if there was anything he could do. I told him no but thanks so much for offering and saving José and Kathy's front door. He told me to come by the dealership the next day and to see if they could fix my door. I looked at my door and realized it looked like my truck had been T-boned by a Prius. This only escalated my anger, not at Michael or Los Nopales, but at Carson and me and the damage we had created from within Los Nopales and to my truck as a result of our behavior.

We left Los Nopales in a cloud of blue smoke like I had just got the green light at East Alabama Drag Strip and have never been back in the restaurant since ... it's too painful. We get it to-go only; it's safer that way!

Within the hour, I was at home, both of us calm, and trying to explain to Mary Lynn what she was bound to hear about in the coming days. The doorbell rang and it was Michael bringing our food in to go containers so we could finish our supper! Ladies and gentlemen, that is follow-through! However, they would not allow him to put the margarita in a to-go cup!

After listening to my story, Mary Lynn calmly asked me why I didn't just simply move to the table Carson wanted to relocate to. The waiter had already said it was ok. BUT, my pride, my fatherly parenting expertise, my manhood ... was being challenged by autism. BUT, BUT, BUT ... she was right ... choose your battles, swallow your selfish pride, and take the necessary steps to de-escalate the situation. While I may have been embarrassed eating in the middle of the restaurant with an arm flapping but *happy* son, it would not have caused near the spectacle that resulted.

To this day, when we go by Los Nopales, Carson will say, "They have a fountain inside ... I'm sorry I flipped that table, George." If only I had heeded what Mary Lynn and the behavioral therapist have said before. Choose your battles and de-escalate at all cost unless someone or he is in danger. By my stubbornness to make a point in a public restaurant, I escalated the situation to a dangerous situation. Stupid George.

Covid 19 and the Pandemic

"This will be over in a couple of weeks, don't fall victim to the hysteria, and there is no way in Hell I'm shutting down my business because of this virus!"

These are statements I made just hours before closing my office (with the exception of emergencies) and the school and community basically shutting down due to the Covid 19 virus spread. Even my church shut its doors to formal worship which I thought would only happen if Hell froze over!

Whatever your opinion of the virus and pandemic, we all experienced a life-changing moment of time similar to The Great Depression, WWII, and 9-11. I'm not trying to quantify or qualify the impact of each event but I simply mean that, retrospectively, the pandemic of 2020 will historically be a "where were you, how did you handle it" event.

It has been said that stress, strain, and trauma expose the weaknesses and flaws in organizations and human behavior. It also allows for strength, hope, faith, and perseverance to shine! Our world and country have been affected by divisiveness, hate, and cultural awareness that has everyone on edge and ready for a fight! Prayerfully, and hopefully, we will all become aware that love conquers all hate, but it has to begin with me (and you).

On the other hand, it has been a time for awareness of the need for us to combine our strengths, despite our differences, in order to make the world a better place for our children. Additionally, despite our best efforts, any amount of planning can be derailed by unexpected events. Very few businesses had "risk of pandemic" on their strategic plans for business interruptions! While families with special needs children might have been prepared for a power outage or snow day, very few were set up or prepared for a sudden shutdown of the routine that would last not days, but *months*.

Personally, the pandemic was an awakening of the future for Mary Lynn, Carson, and me. While Mary Lynn had spent many summers at home with Carson, I was totally unprepared for what "a day in her life" was like. Oh, I had listened to her when I came home from work, but I had not lived the reality of consecutive days and hours of supervision and engagement required when alone with Carson. Many times I was guilty of thinking, "Is it really that bad, why are you in such a bad mood!"

With all due respect to Mary Lynn, she tried to always have something positive to say, but I never realized the toll it could take on a person hour after hour. I had the privilege of going to a job with some predictability, and when I was at home I was usually not alone. It is always easier when support is present. Not surprisingly, I didn't handle this situation very well either.

It seemed like everywhere I turned, the pandemic was wreaking havoc on someone physically or mentally. Mary Lynn and I both had Covid and while we were not deathly ill, we have never felt that bad for that many days! Mentally, Caroline's senior year of high school was filled with disappointment as mile-marker event after event was canceled or extremely scaled down! Both she and Drake's fiancée, Sarah Beth, had their high school and college graduations postponed. While I was secretly dealing with the fact that I still couldn't grasp Carson not going to college with Caroline, Caroline was starting her new chapter in uncharted waters: total virtual classrooms with the college experience. Drake was starting dental school in a "virtual environment' as well. As with everyone, routines were squashed, structure was gone ... it was a weird reality!

On the other hand, it was a wonderful opportunity for quality time with the 3 of us! Boy did I blow that! Instead of focusing on Mary Lynn and Carson, I immersed myself into every virtual seminar or online read I could find to navigate through unemployment portals, Covid 19 protocols, PPE, and EIDL applications! Honestly, looking back, it was the PPE and EIDL applications that really made an ASS of me. I soon realized that my business would be ok but the reality of Carson's situation at home was becoming a fragile mess.

While I never thought he liked going to school, Mary Lynn and I began to realize the structure was necessary for him and worth the battle to get there! I think all parents would agree that we took school structure for granted, but the pandemic helped us appreciate the formality and structure it provides for our children ... and *us!* For special needs families, the organized structure and programs that we all cling to in order to help navigate this world and develop our child were ripped from us!

Carson's behavior began to escalate and eventually mine did too! He didn't understand why people were wearing masks, why we couldn't go to our biweekly restaurant visits, and why I was home all the time. At first, he must have thought summer came early ... a dream for him, a premature challenge for Mary Lynn! The world stopped but autism didn't. It began plowing a deep divide between Carson and me that I felt like had begun to fill in emotionally. Something had to change and we were able to arrange in-home ABA therapy. While there was tremendous value in this thanks to ABA/whisperer Dr. Babcock and Arthur, the behavior continued to escalate. Dr Babcock and Arthur were very gracious to Carson and me and witnessed both Carson and my response to each other. As I observed how they interacted with Carson, I was jealous of their calm demeanor even in Carson's most heated moments.

There were positive moments such as a vacation during the pandemic that was one of the best ever with no protesting from Carson or aggressive departure! There was also the time Carson spontaneously made a stick figure drawing to the family with Mary Lynn being the biggest figure and I was the smallest figure. Was this a message to me? Looking back, it clearly showed how Carson valued Mary Lynn but my relationship with him was in serious jeopardy. There were moments of glory and progress, but the reality of home was different. Something had to change.

The aggression became so bad that I purchased a "batting helmet" to ride in the truck with Carson to prevent the spontaneous blows to my head from rendering me unconscious! These episodes left me raging with anger and having terrible thoughts. Fortunately, the aggression to Mary Lynn was very minimal but the emotional toll was great. In the following chapter, I hope to reveal the positives of the pandemic, but it had to get worse before it got better.

Thank You, Covid 19!

I gave the following speech to my local Chamber of Commerce as we emerged from the pandemic. Although it doesn't have a lot to do with Carson, it has a simple message that I wanted to share from my heart. I may seem cruel, mean, and ignorant in this book, but I'm trying to get better.

I love my family, Carson included, and I love people. Somehow I hope it shows and the Covid 19 era helped put that into perspective for me.... Thank you, Covid 19.

Top 10 Drivers of Patient Satisfaction

Proud Dad moment: Thank you for helping raise my children in this community. My oldest daughter, Allison, and her husband Bo, moved back to LaGrange from Savannah in the Fall of 2018. They moved here because they *wanted* to! Last year, Allison opened the Chicken Salad Chick because she wanted to invest in the community she grew up in! Thank you LaGrange and Troup County for supporting her endeavor and being a community she *wanted* to invest in!

I typically pray every morning for four things related to my career and business: comfortable patients, steady hands, happy staff, and wise choices. My 30 year career as a dentist has been devoted to trying to achieve "clinical excellence" in every case (toot toot).

Recently, I was informed of the top 10 drivers of patient satisfaction. Interestingly, I can only personally control the last two in the list of 10. #9 is *Clinical excellence*, #10 is *Friendliness!* The other 8 drivers of patient satisfaction deal with the performance of our team! So it occurred to me that my daily prayer is accurate (a steady hand and comfortable patient are certainly key to clinical excellence), but that I have spent most of my career devoted to something that is important but not necessarily the reason patients return to our office.

Certainly they want great care but apparently other factors are more important! No matter how good Dr. Gardner, Dr. Higgins, or I may be, patients return for eight additional reasons:

1. How well we work together.

2. Cheerfulness of the office.

3. Response to concerns or complaints.

4. Amount of attention paid to personal and special needs.

5. Staff sensitivity to your concerns.

6. How well we keep you informed.

7. Staff's efforts to include you in treatment decisions.

8. Staff's attitude toward your request.

And yes, I want to recognize the efforts our team makes on a daily basis – and the loyalty you have shown as we have adapted over the past couple of years!

Really, no matter where you work, what you do, or what your skill level is, the people around you are what matters. Staff and Teams, Customers and Clients are all mutually beneficial relationships.

Today, people are nervous, on edge, sensitive, and stressed ... my question is, "Would the world be different if we all started focusing on the top 10 reasons for patient satisfaction?"

Cheerfulness.

Responding appropriately to concerns or complaints.

Pay more attention to each other's needs (everyone has a story you know!).

Be sensitive of other's feelings and opinions.

Communicate clearly and with the proper tone.

Create options to help in decision making.

And finally, our *attitude!!!* Truthfully, a friendly attitude is the only thing we can control consistently!

In conclusion, this all boils down to the two greatest commandments that Jesus was quoted as saying:

1. Love the Lord with all your heart, mind, and soul.
2. Love your neighbor!

If you can't do #1, then for the sake of all of us around you please start doing #2!

Be a positive influence, be the light no matter who or where you are!

Thank you and have a great day!

Hurtful Eyes

In March of 2021, Mary Lynn and I had a conversation that was perhaps a moment that I hope will change *me*. Carson is 24 days shy of 19. He still is aggressive at times and his physical stature and strength can be a force to be reckoned with. He weighs more than me, is slightly taller than me, and has my temper, plus autism ... Mary Lynn's words, not mine!

It has been a particularly rough stretch of mornings as Carson has had loud verbal protest and several acts of physical aggression that have left a mother and a father exhausted and helpless as to what to do next. Nothing unusual for parents of a child with special needs. For that matter, nothing unusual for parents in general. However, as this book has chronicled, we have fought this aggression issue for a long time. The only thing that has changed is Carson's size and the amount of physical damage he is capable of in a short period of time. Most of our pictures are fastened sturdily to the wall with heavy-duty velcro and most of our vases are plastic and filled with artificial flowers that would make any gravesite envious.

Mary Lynn, Allison, and Caroline have a trip planned this weekend for a girls' getaway that was planned pre-Covid. Now, a year later, with destination modifications, they are able to make this much-deserved trip a reality. My response to Carson's verbal protest and aggression to going to school has not been stellar the past couple of weeks ... I have had a setback to my "no returned aggression as a result of aggression" that Arthur and Dr. Babcock have done their best to teach me through ABA therapy with Carson. Instead of looking forward to her trip with her daughters, she is very concerned about leaving Carson with me for the weekend for fear of how I will respond if he becomes aggressive verbally or physically and she is not here to de-escalate me.

Wow, what a punch to the gut for me. The person I love the most in this world and would do anything for has let me know in very kind words that I am not her rock. Instead of looking forward to much-deserved time of respite and quality time with her daughters, she is concerned with how her husband and father of Carson will handle himself this weekend while she is gone.

Now, this is not the first time I've heard this but by the hurt in her eyes I can tell it is wearing her down more than Carson's behavior. You see, despite our prayers and therapy, Carson still has autism. Apparently, that will never go away. Although we have made strides in communication and behavior management, Carson still has handicapping aggression. I keep thinking that despite the size of his testicles, the testosterone level will taper off, but so far it is raging and my experience as a male is it will not subside for many years!

So, I know you see the answer, don't you? If Carson isn't going to change then who needs to change? Yep, Stupid George, the big fat loser! Now my short-term goal is to not engage Carson more, not to curb his aggression, not to make him enjoy going to school. My short-term goal now is to behave more like a loving father despite my son's response to various situations. This sounds like a broken record doesn't it? How many times have I set this goal? Yep, Stupid George is at it again ... you *hypocrite!*

My short-term goal also includes earning Mary Lynn's trust back so that she can simply enjoy some time outside the house without fear of collateral damage from Carson *and me.* No matter how hard you try as a man to provide physically for your family and think you are a rock for those around you, you can ruin the support system in a blink! I need to behave in such a way at all times that those hurtful eyes become joyful eyes.

Springbrook

For several years, Carson has received fantastic care through his psychiatrist, Dr. Sandra Vinson. She treated Carson from about the age of 9 until the age of 19. We had resisted any kind of anti-psychotic meds just because we didn't want Carson's body to deal with that. However, as adolescence was upon us and hormones began to rage, Dr. Vinson strongly encouraged stronger meds in order to help manage Carson.

At one point, when Carson was 15 his behavior reached a point that Mary Lynn and I could not manage it any longer. Carson never said anything violently threatening to us nor did he threaten to harm himself. However, he was becoming more and more physically aggressive with his biting, hitting, and throwing objects when life didn't go his way. Sometimes, it was hard to anticipate but looking back we know most of the behavior was/is an escape mechanism and an attempt on his part to get out of an uncomfortable situation. Therefore, because of a reduced capacity to communicate his concerns, animalistic type behavior becomes the escape mechanism. Then it is a matter of controlling the damage!

Nevertheless, at this point we were desperate for some help and relief. Dr. Vinson recommended we admit Carson to a behavioral hospital for evaluation and medication modification. At that moment, that was the hardest parenting decision we had ever had to make but we did it.

The admission process went well and he willingly went behind the closing door with Mary Lynn and me in tears. We drove home from Atlanta back to LaGrange and it was a very quiet trip; I personally was fighting nausea, and can't speak to what Mary Lynn was feeling but she was quiet and sad. We would miss Christmas with our son. Turns out, we both were envisioning the hysteria, physical damage, and behavior that we were sure he was inflicting on the hospital similar to what we had witnessed at home.

The next morning, we called to check on Carson and to our shock the nurse stated he was very cooperative upon admission and had been the perfect patient: no aggression, just wanted his mom ... gut wrenching! But wait, no aggression? No aggression and he is in a group environment. Ok, so the nurse said this was not unusual and described it as a honeymoon period ... aggression would soon occur. Day two, no aggression, Day three, no aggression — wait, where was this aggressive child?!

Finally, on day four we got a call that we had been waiting for: Carson had been in an "incident" with another child and physical aggression resulted. No one was hurt but they wanted us to be aware. Now the nurse did tell us that Carson did not start the incident and that the other child initiated the aggressive behavior. Additionally (and I believe she chuckled slightly), Carson quickly ended the battle with his returned aggression and had the other child submitting quickly. Redneck Stupid George replied, "Hell, I don't blame him, if you hit me I'm going to hit back. I'm proud of Carson!" I don't think this was appropriate but it felt good to say it.

Carson said every day that he missed his mom ... gut wrenching. On day five we were allowed an in-person visit with Carson and he of course wanted to know when he could go home with Mary Lynn. The visit went well and he exhibited no aggression. At the conclusion of the visit, the nurse told us to check this child out as soon as possible and never bring him back; this was not the place for him. I can't really say why but we trusted her instinct and suggestion. We agreed to keep him there for 48 more hours to be sure he was tolerating a medication change appropriately but we left hopeful for a brighter and hopeful future with Carson. We were dismissed to the care of Dr. Vinson and continued follow-ups with her.

Carson was a new person upon returning home with no aggression, but still with a high level of anxiety. We had learned some techniques to manage this better ... most of all to keep things as low key as possible, especially around the holidays!

For the next few months, it was as if Carson had been "scared straight" and that, with the combination of in-patient care and new meds, we were reaching new heights with Carson. He still had autism, but his engagement, tolerance, and cooperation were improved and very limited amounts of aggression occurred at home. Even at school, things were better.

Fast-forward to March 2020 when the world basically stopped in regard to normal routines, consistency, and predictability. I have already written about the effect of the pandemic and as a result how Carson's behavior began to escalate to new heights. Mostly aggression towards me, even when I was trying Arthur and Dr. Bob techniques. Holes in the sheetrock, lamps broken, aggression toward our pets, Carson was spiraling out of control ... and so was I. No matter how much I tried, when I would be attacked my defense mechanisms would kick in and I would retaliate. I guess he felt that due to my mismanagement of him as a young boy, he now had an obligation to return the favor. And rightfully so, but it crushes me and he is immediately remorseful but the damage is done.

Once again, Mary Lynn and I had a decision to make. We, or at least me, could not continue to live that way ... pins and needles even on good days. We contacted Dr. Vinson and told her we were seeking long-term living options and she said she agreed it was time. She had done all she could do outpatient wise. We researched and found a hospital in South Carolina that specialized in ABA therapy for acute and long term autism-related behavior. They also would be able to assess and change medications safely if needed and also provide therapy services for our family in hopes of bringing Carson back home after some intense in-patient therapy. If this didn't work, I felt like long term-residential care was where we were headed and I knew that would be gut wrenching.

So, after prayers for guidance and tears of sorrow and reluctance, one summer day in July 2021, we took Carson to Springbrook Autism Behavioral Hospital. Again, the transition was smooth considering the circumstances and we sobbed as he gave up his phone, and went behind the closed door with only his security blanket and a teddy bear ... and of course clothes. He was escorted by two large black males that were so strong yet so chill and comforting. As Mary Lynn and I walked to the car one of them came out and reassured us he was in good hands and they would love him! We called daily but were not allowed to see him for two weeks other than a Zoom call. The most comforting call was at night after he had gone to bed and we would talk to his nurse and she would report on his day.

Unlike the previous in-patient visit, it didn't take long for the aggression to begin. Basically, Carson raised hell and wanted to go home. We would tell him on the phone that we were having the house repaired from the broken doors and damaged sheetrock and that it was going to take a while. We anticipated a two- to four-week stay but this time we were committed to seeing the process through. This was critical for Carson to be able to come home.

While our other children had moved out, they visited quite often and now we had a *grandbaby!* Carson was not quite sure how to respond to the grandbaby, but I couldn't take a chance with his elevated aggression. We had to get control of this issue or he couldn't come home. The condition for him to live at home was for us to be able to have immediate family over on occasion for low-key events that Carson could chose to participate in or not. Also, the spontaneous aggression over the slightest event had to stop. Not much to ask.... Mary Lynn and I prayed daily for a calm spirit to overwhelm Carson and allow him to reach a peaceful place.

At our first Zoom conference with the doctor, the doctor stated he had not seen an individual with such a high level of social anxiety. He said Carson was "off the chart" with anxiety and acute intervention would be necessary. The treatment plan called for complete medication changes to reduce the anxiety and then begin intensive ABA therapy. Mary Lynn and I constantly had Carson on our mind. Was he being cared for? Was he crying and screaming all the time? Was he eating? Was he sleeping? Did he lay awake at night and wonder if we would ever come get him?

It was painful but as the days went by we developed a peace about the decision as we talked most days with the nurses and therapist and realized he was making progress.

The two- to four-week time frame turned in to a four-month stay as Carson continued to improve. The therapist also worked with us via Zoom on interacting with Carson and with me on my response to Carson's behavior. The hardest part was after the two-week no-visit policy, we would be allowed an in-person visit, but Covid was making another comeback and the facility implemented a no-visit policy for six weeks! Mary Lynn and I stayed busy doing things we weren't able to do when Carson was at home such as spontaneously visiting our kids and going out to eat.

We traveled to Greenville every other weekend just to feel closer to Carson even though we couldn't visit in person. When we were finally able to see him, he had a full beard, which we knew from the Zoom calls, but were pleasantly surprised at how good he looked and the weight he had lost. I will not bore you with the details of therapy, but suffice it to say that we wished we had done this earlier! Visits came more often in the next six weeks and Carson tolerated us leaving better each time with no aggression.

When he was dismissed from the program, he had lost 44 pounds, had two scars from bites from other clients, but otherwise looked great! We had been kept well informed of any incidences and felt great about the care he had received. Interestingly, he was off *all* anti-psychotic meds and was only taking an anti-depressant and anti-anxiety meds.

Now, for the true test: the return home. Carson was a complete gentleman for the four-hour trip home. He had earned his phone back and could keep it as long as he didn't use it as a weapon! He was so relaxed to be home. He was like a different man ... still had autism, still needed reassurance and consistency, but a different man.

Thanksgiving was very low key but he tolerated the immediate family wonderfully, including the grandbaby.

Next test, school. When the morning came to start back to high school, he showed increased anxiety and stated he wasn't going to school. We calmly told him his teacher wanted to see him and it was the same teacher from last year ... although we had lost Arthur and a new behavioral technician awaited Carson. I told Carson he could go to school at "camp" (Springbrook) or he could go to school at Troup High and live with Mom. He quickly responded, "I will go to Troup High School" and immediately began to get ready!

The transition back to school went well and after the first week back his teacher and the lead ABA therapist commented that this was a different young man! It was as if someone opened his brain and rewired it with reduced anxiety and increased tolerance for transition. Prayers answered (praise the Lord) and several months of great peace occurred in the Childress household.... We can live like this!

The Exceptional Way

I want to be a part of something bigger than myself that impacts lives for the positive. Having a child with special needs has opened my eyes to a world with un-met needs. While many programs exist that foster the development and relationships for children with special needs, the transition to adulthood presents new challenges in this area.

Since Carson was reaching this transition age, Mary Lynn and I were considering what our next steps would be in regards to a structured day for Carson. As Mary Lynn and I began to look at post-high school options, we became acutely aware of a lack of quality programs in our area to meet this growing need. Therefore, we, along with several other families committed to developing a day program for these adults.

After many months of planning and team efforts, The Exceptional Way, LLC was formed. Its purpose will strive to "fill the gap" for adults with special needs to foster relationship development and recreational activities in this expanding population.

The following is the story on how The Exceptional Way, LLC became organized and is copied directly from our website: theexceptionalway.org.

> Years ago, three mothers began an emotionally complex journey when their sons were diagnosed with cognitive and developmental delays. The mothers are Jodi, Laurie, and Mary Lynn and are affectionately known as the "momma bears."
>
> Like many other parents of children with special needs, they knew they would spend an exceptional amount of time navigating the children through a world that can be exceedingly difficult for a person with disabilities. They also believed that *everyone* deserves a life of meaning and purpose based around relationships with other people. Of all the emotional needs in life, the most constant is love. The harder emotions abound when you can't heal your child or "fix" the problem in a world that doesn't always em-

brace "different" or "challenged." However, because of the unconditional love we all have for our children, these mothers know their children need a place to belong and be a part of something bigger!

The school system can provide tremendous services to these individuals until the age of 22 when the services are discontinued and a big gap occurs for social and intellectual development in our community. For children with intellectual or developmental issues, the end of high school does not necessarily signify the beginning of a promising and fulfilling future. In reality, it often represents a future of continually finding a place to belong or participate in. It is the end of a comfortable, familiar support system of friends, teachers and mentors which have been provided for years through the school system.

The mothers know that relationship development and community involvement is critical for everyone, including their sons! These mothers have a dream for their sons and other underserved individuals like them in our community. After months of research and field visits to similar programs in other cities, our Board is announcing the formation of The Exceptional Way, Inc. Our mission is to provide a day program and facility in Troup County to promote social and relationship development along with community involvement for adults with special needs. Additionally, the well-being of the families will be enriched knowing their loved one can thrive through these activities.

The Exceptional Way, Inc. has received 501c3 status and is now actively seeking funds for our initial capital efforts. Will you consider being a part of our dream becoming a reality and contribute to this much needed service in Troup County?

theexceptionalway.org

Due to Carson's aggression history, he currently will not qualify for the program as it exists today, but I still have embraced this project because I see the impact it has on the families and individuals that attend. So much joy occurs every day and for now, a small group of individuals benefit from the fledgling program. It is my goal that this will grow and be able to serve many families with varying levels of needs.

Come see us someday! Most of all, write us a check please!

Conclusion

Carson just turned 21 and this was our conversation that evening: "Wanna beer ... no thank you!" Twin sister: "No, I'll have a martini."

Leading up to Spring break was full of optimism and hope with the family getting together. Mary Lynn, Carson, and I had a great trip down to Cape San Blas ... no crowds, just raw beach and bay – despite three traffic jams and a seven hour trip time, no aggression. Our reservation was for seven days.

Day one: boat trip in the bay ... hot tub enjoyed. Grand baby Evans arrived Sunday night and Carson tolerated all the guests well.

Day two: boat ride again and this time Carson asked if he could snorkel ... just Carson and me but plenty of great video to document the moment – no aggression!

Day three: Carson woke up and asked to go home. Things escalated quickly, his aggression escalated, and we made the decision to return home and leave the others to enjoy the remaining time. Tears of joy for the moments we had with them and Carson, and tears of sadness with the emotional letdown of plans thwarted.

Turns out Mary Lynn had anticipated leaving at day four but of course I had hoped for day six! Neither of us planned on day three.

I had hoped by the end of this book I would be able to write about a miraculous healing, incredible social skill development, and total engagement with the rest of the family, but I can't. Carson still has autism and still has anxiety which manifests with aggression. He is better but each day brings some type of challenge. He has definitely developed and we all look back and realize how far we have come!

In the words of Churchill, "We (Mary Lynn and I, married for 36 years) will *never, ever* give up!" I know Churchill said more "nevers" and "evers," but damn I'm tired.

My hope and prayer for you as a parent or guardian of a special needs child is that you will have the love and support of loved ones around you in this journey and the stamina to thrive. And if you are extended family, neighbor, or friend of a special needs child or family, you will provide encouragement, physical and emotional support, and occasional respite for these courageous families. And for God's sake if you are a father to a special needs child, suck it up, be a man, and provide emotionally, physically, financially, and be engaged as much as you can!

Be present!!!!

Do the *best* you can and know that you will fail at times ... and that's ok! Also, remember Mom and Dad, the *Holy Spirit* and a little red wine can make the worst day better! And if your Southern Baptist friends judge you for the red wine (tequila/rum/bourbon), ask them how many pills they take for anxiety or depression!

Finally, love the Lord with all your heart, mind, and soul ... and just as important, "Huff" (love) your neighbor. And if all else fails, ask to be buried face down so the rest of the world can kiss your ass!

Wait a minute, that's not how I want to be remembered. That still sounds bitter and resentful and as if I haven't grown in my desire to be more tolerant and loving to the world around me. If all else fails, take care of those around you, suck it up, move on, and don't do anything to tarnish the family name!

Love y'all,
Stupid George ... the big fat loser.
Tarnished but transparent.

About the Author

DR. GEORGE W. CHILDRESS is a native of Roanoke, Alabama but now calls LaGrange, Georgia his home after residing there for 32 years. He is a graduate of Auburn University (B.S., 1986) and the University of Alabama (Birmingham) School of Dentistry (D.M.D., 1991).

Dr. Childress has been active in the community through various volunteer organizations and is a Sunday School teacher at First Baptist Church on the Square where he also volunteers at the "Free Dental Clinic." Professionally, he has achieved Fellowship status with the Academy of General Dentistry and is one of 10 dentists in the state of Georgia that has achieved accreditation status with the American Academy of Cosmetic Dentistry.

Most importantly, George has been married for 36 years to the former Mary Lynn Page of LaGrange and they have four children and two "in-law" children, Allison (Bo), Drake (Sara Beth), Carson, and Caroline. Additionally, Bo and Allison have blessed them with their first grandchild, Evans, and they have another on the way!

George can be reached at *george@drchildress.com* and welcomes your thoughts and feedback.

• Exceptional Press •

www.ingramcontent.com/pod-product-compliance
Lightning Source LLC
LaVergne TN
LVHW020654100826
845148LV00012B/2496